GAME TIME

HOW TO ORDER THIS BOOK

BY PHONE: 800-233-9936 or 717-291-5609, 8AM–5PM Eastern Time

BY FAX: 717-295-4538

BY MAIL: Order Department
Technomic Publishing Company, Inc.
851 New Holland Avenue, Box 3535
Lancaster, PA 17604, U.S.A.

BY CREDIT CARD: American Express, VISA, MasterCard

BY WWW SITE: http://www.techpub.com

GAME TIME
THE EDUCATOR'S PLAYBOOK FOR THE NEW GLOBAL ECONOMY

Leon M. Lessinger, Ed.D.
Consultant/Educator
Florida Eminent Scholar, Education Policy & Economic Development
Senior Fellow, Florida Institute of Education
(State University System)

Allen E. Salowe, MBA, AICP
Consultant/Educator
Senior Fellow, Florida Institute of Education
(State University System)
Senior Fellow, Florida Center for Electronic Communications
(State University System)

TECHNOMIC
PUBLISHING CO., INC.
LANCASTER · BASEL

Game Time

a **TECHNOMIC** publication

Published in the Western Hemisphere by
Technomic Publishing Company, Inc.
851 New Holland Avenue, Box 3535
Lancaster, Pennsylvania 17604 U.S.A.

Distributed in the Rest of the World by
Technomic Publishing AG
Missionsstrasse 44
CH-4055 Basel, Switzerland

Printed in the United States of America
10 9 8 7 6 5 4 3 2 1

Main entry under title:
    Game Time: The Educator's Playbook for the New Global Economy

A Technomic Publishing Company book
Bibliography: p.

Library of Congress Catalog Card No. 97-60629
ISBN No. 1-56676-542-0

CONTENTS

Chapter 8: Solutions – Work Force Development and Winning   163

Chapter 9: Guidelines for Building the Playbook for Education   183

MORE THAN ANY other sport, football lends itself to myth and folklore. In the 75-year history of the National Football League (and its predecessors), some mighty large specimens, a few as legendary as Paul Bunyon, have learned and relearned how to play the game of football at the pinnacle of achievement—*professional* football.

Through stories, you get a glimpse into the game of football itself and are able to relate to our principal message: global economic change, fierce rivalry, thinking, and learning a living. The sport has a bit of everything, from the poetry of life to the brutality of competition. When you look at players in the trenches, you grasp the psychology of the game. It is organized warfare.

Every fall, there is a new season in professional football. Teams assemble with the high expectations of having a winning season. The past for them and their leaders is not a prologue to the future. Losers can and do become winners.

Every fall, there is a new season in America's schools and on its college campuses. Faculties and administrators assemble. Can the football spirit and mindset also prevail off of the field? It doesn't now. But it can, and should. We show why and how.

Our basic premise is that sports, especially NFL football, is the nation's communicator of key ideas. It is a powerful metaphor for understanding the world of change beyond the stadium and practice fields.

- The games during the season—and from season to season—are all different. Football shows adjustment to change.
- When the new league season starts, no outcome is impossible.

Sunday after Sunday, the battle is a new one, and another chance for glory.

- The roster is separated into *offensive* (breakthrough) and *defensive* (control) squads, which are teams within teams. The mindset of the defense is different from the strategy of the offense.
- Breakthrough is not the same as control, but both are critical to a team's success.
- Professional football is a game of specialists. The quarterback and the coaches plus the team captains—players and mentors—are the leaders of the team.
- Players demonstrate the essence of football, working together as a system of players. The kicking team—the center, ball holder, and kicker—show the essence of working together as a sub-system of players.

The "bible" of an NFL team and the pro football player is an unimpressive loose-leaf notebook called the *playbook*. It is dog-eared from constant use and updating. It is provided to each player by his head coach. It is, in fact, a continuously improved job description. In it is distilled all the knowledge essential to the proper execution of his assignments.

It is not an easy book to master. It requires continuous learning to demonstrate continuous improvement. Some pro teams have as many as 300 offensive plays. None of the plays on offense or defense work perfectly unless every player on the field (and those waiting on the sidelines to play if suddenly called upon) performs his duty.

Each play sheet describes the duties of each position on every play. During the season, depending on how well the play works against various defenses in the league, changes are made by the coaches. The variations are entered into each playbook. The playbook is valuable property. When a player is traded or cut, his playbook is picked up. The loss of a playbook can cost a player, in fines, a great deal of money.

NFL teams are so closely matched that, often enough, the newcomer team wallops the champion. In their second season, both the expansion Carolina Panthers and Jacksonville Jaguars, for example, reached the playoff finals in their respective conference putting them only one game away from a trip to Super Bowl XXXI.

The Carolina Panthers proved to be the most successful new franchise in NFL history and their coach, Don Capers, was chosen as 1996 NFL Coach of the Year. Causes are many, but one is preeminent. This is the phenomenon of the free agent.

Finally, the success of a play, a game, or a season often comes down to the individual efforts of one player. There are no excuses for failure.

Woven throughout this book are six themes that apply to NFL success as well as serving as models for schools and enterprise to improve their performance on the competitive playing fields of a new, information-driven, global economy. Its messages:

(*1*) Ophelimity thinking—This is customer-centered quality. In football, the fan is king; in business, it's the customer. In schools, it should be the student.

(*2*) Praxis makes perfect—We know and show what works in the playbook. Educators, managers, workers, and NFL players are professionals.

(*3*) American *kaizen*—Continuous improvement links breakthrough and control (small steps open big opportunities) for teachers, workers, and managers.

(*4*) Technology—The support element to American *kaizen*. The new "tools of the trade" change the way the game is played.

(*5*) Coopetition—Teamwork and competition. In a global economy, it is not either/or, but both.

(*6*) Leadership—It comes together in Learning Commonwealths. Putting continuous learning first assures the rest will follow.

The idea for this work first saw light during a series of discussions between the authors following one of the Frederick A. Schultz-sponsored lectures held at the University of North Florida in Jacksonville. Former Secretary of Labor Ray Marshall had come to address business and education leaders. He spoke of what we have now come to think of and call "an iron link" between learning and America's success in the new global economy. Dr. Marshall and Marc Taylor in their thought provoking book, *Thinking for a Living: Education and the Wealth of Nations,* write, "The key to both productivity and competitiveness is the skills of our people and our capacity to use highly educated and trained people to maximum advantage in the workplace."

That day, the clear and compelling message was aimed directly at the audience responsible for creating wealth in our economy: educators and business executives. Its content neither fell on deaf ears nor on a group unfamiliar with its underlying arguments. However, what seemed needed was an action focus, a playbook to help business leaders and educators quickly understand, build, and adapt to the changes converging upon them from an emerging information-rich global economy.

Over the next two years, this book, *Game Time: The Educator's Playbook for the New Global Economy,* took shape. It brought together these insights into an uncomplicated model for action. The words and ideas are aimed at the general reader with particular emphasis on policy makers and educators anxious to explore the implications of the iron link between schools and jobs and to take proactive steps for achieving measurable results in learning and improvements in worker earning.

The message was periodically tested and received fresh momentum through workshop papers presented to, and discussions among, business and education leaders. Especially valuable were roundtable meetings involving leading educators and CEOs of both large and small businesses in Florida sponsored by Enterprise Florida, a public-private business consortium that includes the Florida Jobs and Education Partnership and the Florida Department of Education.

The issues are clearly and repeatedly voiced. America is increasingly caught up in a series of unprecedented global economic activities. A gradual awareness of changes needed in U.S. education is out there, but there exists little coordinated practical wisdom to make the changes. By default, it has fallen to business leaders, supported by technology investments, to take on the central role of bringing about the needed skills and performance improvements for the entire U.S. work force—to "think and work smarter" in an information-rich, *cognitive economy,* which is based on *human capital*—men and women capable of thinking, reasoning, and problem solving.

The goal is to help the reader grasp why there is, more so than ever, this iron link between learning and wealth creation, and how to think and act smarter about it.

ACKNOWLEDGEMENTS

AN EARLY MONOGRAPH on this subject, *Coopetition: Cooperative Competition: How to Gain and Keep Wealth in the New American Economy,* was critiqued by Pat Sager, A.B.D., North Florida Regional Director for Webster University. Her insights and action focus stimulated important changes in the thrust of our presentation. Pat reflects one of the "new breed" of professional educators—what we called in the book, an Era 3 Pioneer. She contributed the concept of "Flexibility into Immediacy," which captured the proactive mindset necessary to seize opportunities as well as face down and solve the pressing problems. Together with Dr. Baraz Simiian, Director of Academic Affairs and Professor of Organizational Behavior and Leadership at Webster University, the comments led directly to using the sports metaphor in the final text.

An early draft manuscript was carefully reviewed and commented upon by Jay R. Wilson, Vice President and Investment Banker at J. P. Morgan, New York. Jay's detailed written margin notes stimulated further discussions, leading directly to a strong "bottom line" orientation for the overarching concepts of the book.

A special word of thanks to Dr. Donn (yes, double "d" is correct) V. Kaupke, Superintendent of Schools, Flagler County, Florida. An educator and ex-football player, he summed up the following pages with, "First you teach your players to execute, then you play the game. . . . To educate our youth is to assure our representative democracy is kept whole." And, Carolyn Wehle, a newly minted Masters in Educational Counseling, immediately applied the metaphor as a means of better reaching high school students with complex subject matter.

Janet McGinley was one of our most severe critics, always forcing the authors to make it read more understandably. Cynthia Beard assumed the reading role of "the every person" in her manuscript critique. Both of these ladies added immeasurably to any improved readability of the final drafts.

Our grateful thanks go to these reviewers whose contributions helped result in a better finished work. However, they should in no way be held responsible for any of its shortcomings.

CHAPTER 1

A Winning Perspective

FORMER AMBASSADOR TO Russia Robert Strauss liked to start his presentation this way: "Before I begin," he said, "I have something to say." Before you get deep into this book, we want to make several points.

We chose the title of our book to be *Game Time: The Educator's Playbook for the New Global Economy,* because we wanted to show how a discussion of American professional sports—particularly football—lights up the dark corners of obstacles to becoming successful in today's changing economy.

We are *optimists-by-design*—pragmatists who seek answers, not excuses, to problems. We know that in professional sports, every season is a new season, with new opportunities for winning. In every season, there is a new *playbook,* revised to take advantage of what has been learned and what may have changed.

In football, there is no single magic playbook. If there were, everyone would run the same plays all of the time. There is no magic way to do things. There are so many ways to do things.

Our book is intended as a thoughtful guide to praxis, to "what works" to meet the tough situations brought on by the fierce competitive global economy that now has become both an enemy and a source of opportunity.

POINT OF VIEW

We have entered an era of man-made brainpower industries. Individual, corporate, and national economic success all require new and more extensive sets of brainpower-derived human skills, a form of pragmatic intellectual capital, more than had been required in either the first era of civilization, the Agricultural Age, or the second era, the Industrial Age.

By themselves, skills, a form of intellectual capital, do not guarantee success in a global economy. They are, as the scientists say, necessary but not sufficient. Human skills have to be put together in successful organizations, a task that itself depends on new exercises in brainpower. But without human skills—what economists call *human capital*—there are no successful, competitive organizations in the new global economy.

Today, companies have the ability to make anything, anywhere in the world, and then sell and deliver it anywhere else in the world. Knowledge and skill have become the only source of long-run sustainable, competitive advantage. Transportation and communication technologies mean that highly skilled workers in one place, what can be described as the *first world,* can work effectively with the unskilled in the *third world.*

A company, or a country, today puts together its first-world-type workers who qualify for higher wages with lower-waged, third-world-type workers wherever they can be assembled. The advantage? This arrangement cuts costs and spurs profits, without loss of quality. Today, workers are paid for their skills, not as they were once paid, for the skills of those who were in the same place physically.

Put bluntly, in today's emerging global economy, men and women with third-world skills can only earn third-world wages even if they live in the first world. Viewed more accurately, unskilled labor can be, and is, bought wherever it is cheapest and readily available.

The implication for America's education systems, given this economic reality, is obvious. Companies can find the skilled, or those easier and cheaper to learn skills, wherever they exist in the world. They do not have to hire an American high school graduate who, all too typically, is not a world-class worker. His or her educational deficits are not the employer's problem. From an economic standpoint, why should a company invest in the costly effort of giving a new employee the now necessary market skills when they can get what they need from a well-prepared Chinese, Russian, or Indonesian high school graduate?

Until the early 1970s, a truly global economy did not exist. Unskilled Americans, simply by virtue of being American and fortunate enough to work alongside those with higher skills in settings equipped with the needed capital and raw materials, were in the right place at the right time. As such, they could get good wages. That situation has changed drastically. Americans have to direct their thinking to this threat to our economic well-being quickly and effectively. Our economic opponents, located throughout the rest of the world, have targeted the products and markets of our most successful enterprises. Even if we decide not to have an offensive program, we must shore up our defenses.

What is true in sports is especially true now for our economic security: if one plays defense all the time and one is never on offense, one never wins.

PROFESSIONAL FOOTBALL

Whether or not your favorite team becomes champion of the National Football League (NFL) will depend on what happens down on the field on autumn Sunday afternoons or Monday nights in stadiums around the league.

Each week, there will be cheerleaders and bands and upwards of 70,000 screaming fans looking on from their seats.

It's game time!

But the outcome of that game and the ones to come will be determined long before the crowd files into the stands and the television cameras roll.

The difference between victory and defeat, barring the flukes of chance, will depend on what first takes place on a simple patch of grass, sometimes adjacent to the stadium. It is surrounded by a functional looking chain-link fence shrouded with black tarpaulin for security and a few portable bleachers. It is there, away from the stadium glitter and lights, that the success of your team will, in large part, be determined. It is where the opportunity for a future Super Bowl ring is first measured.

On that patch of grass there will be sweat, hits, and endless repetition. Success starts quietly. The backbone of the winning team is forged in the seemingly endless hours of practice, practice, and still more practice.

In the 1960s, football was a different game. Television money was just starting to trickle in, and free agents were still almost 3 decades away. In that year, the Atlanta Falcons franchise, for example, had just been bought, at what today is a bargain price.

Things weren't very fancy that first year. The Falcons' player training camp was set up in an out-of-the-way summer church camp in the North Carolina mountains. There was reportedly a "small" problem. There were no football fields, no lockers, no showers.

The new owner solved the problem by landscaping a large cow pasture, then marking it off with chalk lines, and putting up goal posts. At least it now "looked" like a football field. The plumber came to install a shower room. But, lacking proper drainage, the runoff flowed through the shed's front door.

The spartan surroundings not only saved money, but hardened the players for the upcoming season. Their buses were worn out Greyhounds, and one reportedly had no top. By the time they arrived at their first exhibition game, the players looked as though they had already been through a battle.

Each new season marks a new beginning. It's a chance to put past losses in perspective, behind us, and to wipe the slate clean. Last year's winners can't rest on their laurels. Last year's losers are not preordained to repeat last year's mistakes. Both winners and losers face new opportunities and new challenges on a fast, ever-changing, playing field.

Each team does its homework. The more purposeful usually do better. Those who scout the "new look" of other teams and ready themselves for the battle are more prepared to dominate the game as well as adapt to game time surprises. The game keeps moving faster, constantly changing with the improved physical and mental skills of the players and the experiences of the coaches.

Each year, the team's playbook must be rewritten. The old plays may have worked before—some can still be used intact—but some are now stale, out of date with new realities. They have been scouted by the other teams. The strategy, the tactics, and the deception—the art of surprise—must be reinvented again and again.

How did it all begin?

Professional football began in a decade of restlessness brought on by intense change. It answered a need for violence. Like the present, the 1920s were turbulent years. Professional football was sired by that turbulence. Young men fresh from a world war needed a socially acceptable outlet for their emotions. They found it in pro football; some as players, most as spectators.

In the small towns of America, even before the 1920s, pro teams had flourished briefly, and then died. The legend of Jim Thorpe was strong, but it was the persistence of Curly Lambeau that kept both pro football and his team, the Green Bay Packers alive. He organized the team with $500 put up by the packing company. The players passed the hat after the game to earn some money. One season, each player's share came to $16.75.

The club survived. In the violent change-instigated climate of the 1920s, pro football began to prosper. The restless young men began to come in a steady stream. They played for the great football dynasties — the Packers, the Bears, the Eagles, and the Giants. They built pro football so solidly that it was ready when another violent change interval — the post World War II period — arrived in the 1950s. New teams were organized, and new leagues started up.

Today, the teams that once traveled in ramshackle buses to play before a handful of people fly by chartered jets to perform before crowds of customers that sometimes exceed 100,000. Through television, the pro game enters homes in every city, town, and hamlet in the country, indeed, in the world. And all this seems to be just the beginning as we can see by the new franchises, the constant bidding by communities for teams, and the building of more elaborate stadiums.

Football has now surpassed baseball as America's national sport.

WHAT CAN WE LEARN FROM PROFESSIONAL SPORTS?

> Insight #1—Recognition of the supreme importance of *human capital*

The first president of the (NFL) was Bert Bell. As much as any man, he was responsible for the filled stands of customers — fans. Bert both played and coached football. He designed and implemented the league policy on television that made pro football the fastest growing professional sport in the United States.

His fundamental approach to the essence of the game is represented by the following remark to a reporter: "The one thing we can't forget is that this game was built and made popular by the players. We owe them everything. I don't think that any group of athletes in the world can match pro football players for honesty and character and strength."

Teamwork is a feature of human capital development. The constant winners in football display a near-perfect combination of speed, power, and versatility that comes from the bonds formed among the players forged through teamwork. Years of working together and facing the climate pressure that is the life of every player have made the regulars almost intuitive in their knowledge of each other's reactions. They both compete and collaborate with one another (the hallmark of coopetition) — the competition is to be better, the collaboration exists when the team is at game time.

The success of a play, a game, or a season very often comes down to the individual effort of one player. To no one is this more apparent than the safetyman, whose mistakes cost touchdowns, not just yards.

The game goes on despite rain or snow or mud. Baseball players get a day off if it rains; the football player hunches his shoulders so that the back of his helmet will protect his neck from the cold, wet, and plays. Mud is not really an equalizer; the better team wins in the mud as it would win on a dry field.

Insight #2—The continuous use and upgrading of technology

The football helmet is one example of football's constant employment of technology both as things and processes. The first helmet was merely a good growth of long hair. The early helmets covered the hair with soft, thin leather that fitted snugly and transmitted the shock of a blow almost undiluted.

As the game matured and the science of protection progressed with it, the helmets were changed. The leather used was hard leather padded inside. The change helped, but the driving shock of a knee on the side of the helmet, for example, could not be absorbed by such a device.

John T. Riddell developed the prototype of the modern helmet — a plastic shell suspended on webbing. It could absorb far more impact. The initial shock of the blow was distributed over the webbing so that there was no dangerous localized impact. All helmets now use the suspension principle. It is safe to say that any football helmet today offers its wearer virtually complete protection from blows to the head.

Insight #3—The importance of a team's shared vision of its purpose

---

Pro football teams develop by design a sort of corporate "personality." Over the years, regardless of personnel, a team will exhibit a personality in itself.

During the 1940s for example, perhaps the toughest personality in the NFL was the Philadelphia Eagles. Their coach was a tough man named Greasy Neale. He imprinted his team with that toughness. Greasy was an uncomplicated man. He taught an uncomplicated offense and defense based on the theory that the best way to advance or protect the football is to knock down everyone in the way.

The Eagles in their heyday had only a few plays. They weren't fancy, but they worked. The Eagles won a divisional title in 1947 and world championships in 1948 and 1949. In most recent times, teams like the Raiders and the Steelers, to name only two, have distinct "personalities."

Insight #4—Football exhibits the attractiveness of diversity

Save for talent, there is no discrimination in playing for the NFL. The explosion of interest in professional football among the customers and the shear devotion to the game crosses ethnic, racial, social, economic, and intellectual lines. Top executives are season ticket holders along with employees from all ranks and status. A good percentage of any pro football crowd is made up of women. The kids come by the thousands.

Insight #5—Football puts a premium on excellent two-way communication

Seldom has an enterprise and a medium for its presentation meshed so neatly as pro football and television. An apt expression is to call football *telegenic.*

The owners of the teams are highly sensitive to fan communication. So are the players.

The TV representatives play their roles superbly. The games are presented crisply, colorfully, and accurately, without bias. The announcers and color men and women, as often as not, are outstanding ex-players. They can point up and convey the violent "charm" and intricacies of the game perfectly.

TV makes *game time* familiar to the nation. The sport has become the leading metaphor for conveying innumerable other ideas.

Insight #6—Football shows what leaders need to inspire and manage specialists

---

Professional football is a game for specialists. The men who play it can do one thing or a combination of a few things superlatively well. In this gallery of stars, only one does a number of different things very, very, well. He is the loneliest man in football and the leader of the team: the quarterback.

Ideally, he passes with the instinctive accuracy of a fabled Kentucky rifleman, fakes as coolly as the operator of a carnival shell game, and runs as thoughtfully as a fox before an English hunting party. He must know all the complexities of the modern pro offense faultlessly, and he must command this wide range of knowledge instantly. He must inspire his teammates and dazzle them with his daring and finesse.

Not all quarterbacks can be this ideal; they all have working models they can relate to and emulate.

Insight #7—Football illustrates the critical importance of breakthrough and control

---

In football, as in battle, the surest way to success is to outmaneuver the enemy to penetrate and to secure what has been won. These are the concepts of *breakthrough* and *control*.

Every winning coach, from time to time, wonders what he is really there for. Coaches wear many hats, of course. The executive role calls for three: leader, manager, and administrator. As leaders, coaches motivate and supply the emotional and spiritual necessities of command and inspiration. As administrators, they communicate and enforce the necessary rules and regulations. As managers, they are concerned primarily with the ways their team can achieve breakthrough (offense) and control (defense).

The greatest NFL coaches are teachers. They teach you how to play the game. They point out when things go well. They point out when things do not go so well. Their greatest thrill is to watch the players come together as a team, as a bonding force.

Football is a controlled form of warfare. Offense is dynamic, decisive movement for penetration—hopefully to score. The military words for this breakthrough are invasion, attack, and charge. Defense means control. The military words for control are dig in, stand fast, and hold the line.

The strategy for penetration in warfare includes such concepts as mobility, surprise, deception, and maneuver. It includes seizing the momentum. These are precisely what are used in football. Passing provides an excellent example.

The best launchers of the air attack have a disregard for the consequences that attend the successful catch. The best players orient their whole body to the ball and completely concentrate on it. They focus on the ball regardless of the "punishment" they may receive by a defender. Pass catching is a complicated, demanding trade. It encompasses trickery, good acting on fakes, and an encyclopedic knowledge of the defensive players in the league.

The equipment for breakthrough includes bomber planes, parachutists to drop behind the lines, landing craft, and tanks. Small wonder that in the parlance of football one finds such terms as blitz, bombs (for passes), and tanks (for men of huge stature).

In contrast, the conceptual approach for defense consists of entrenchment, fortification, and detection. Here, the men on the line are vital. Someone has described the yard of space that separates the offensive line from the defensive one in pro football as "no man's land." It is an apt description; football games are won or lost by control of this narrow slip of land. The battle for it is a violent one. It is fought by the biggest, strongest athletes in the sports world.

An especially important leadership fact emerges from the study of breakthrough and control. They are part of one continuing cycle of events. The cycle consists of alternating plateaus and gains in performance. The gains are the result of breakthrough—planned creation of change. The plateaus are the result of control—prevention of change. This goes on and on.

Lurking behind this simple truth are some very profound differences. In terms of leadership and management, control differs remarkably from breakthrough. Successful coaches are fully aware that the attitudes, the organization, and the methodology used to achieve breakthrough differ in essence from those used to achieve control. The differences in fact are so great that the decision of whether, at any one time, to embark on breakthrough, or to continue on control, is of cardinal importance. We shall see this clearly in the discussion of enterprises seeking planned change and/or stability.

The invader must be capable of boldness, cunning, decisiveness, risk taking, and timing. The defender emphasizes patience, alertness, suspicion, and caution.

Insight #8—Football illustrates the fundamental principle of *continuous improvement* as the hallmark of a successful organization

---

Terry Bradshaw was the first player chosen in the 1970 NFL draft. The Pittsburgh Steelers needed a star quarterback; but his early career was anything but successful.

In his first career regular season game, Bradshaw completed four of sixteen passes, and during his freshman season he threw at least three interceptions in seven different games.

"I was totally unprepared for pro football. I had no schooling on reading defenses, I never studied game films the way a quarterback should. In college I simply overpowered the opposition."

Bradshaw obviously had the athletic ability to be a success in the NFL, but during that rookie season many doubted his mental approach to the game. He scrambled all over the field and threw the ball for interceptions. Some sports writers wrote about him being dumb. Bradshaw wasn't certain how much credence Steelers' Head Coach Chuck Noll gave these smears. Six games into the 1974 season, Noll called him over and assured him. "Go make your mistakes. We're going to win with you." It was the turning point of Terry Bradshaw's career.

"Mistakes we'll make. Mistakes we'll overcome. The most important thing is to fly right and have some fun."—Steelers Coach Bill Cowher

---

Training in football is never-ending both before, during, and after the season. The "ordeal" of a pro football rookie shows clearly the critical importance of continuous learnng through guided practice. Players come from all parts of the nation. They are brash, bashful, quiet, loud, tall, short. All of them are strong and quick and very skillful at their trade. Their chance of continuing to practice that trade is small indeed, since at best only three or four of the thirty-odd rookies in a pro training camp will make the team.

Some of them are college All-Americans, fresh from the best year of their lives. Others played on small college teams, before small crowds, and the big city is a new and frightening experience. The rookies are nervous and subdued, while the old pros chat easily about the season coming and the season past.

In the first scrimmage, the rookie finds out that the pros are even bigger and faster and tougher than he had feared. The veterans are fighting for their jobs, too. They fight with guile and power. It is not enough to be brave and quick; everyone on this team is. There's a plus quality of toughness of mental fiber and mental agility that makes the final difference.

For the rookie who makes the team, a new trial begins. Mistakes that were condoned in practice or in exhibition games draw quick and bitter censure now from teammates and coaches. The arsenal of plays that arms a pro team on offense or defense is staggering. It takes long hours of study for the rookie to master assignments that have become second nature to the old pros on the team.

Then there are the technical subtleties of football, the techniques of blocking and tackling and running that college coaches lacked the time or the knowledge to explain. There is, too, the never-ending study of the players on the other teams. The rookie becomes a member of a team within a team. For a while, he'll probably play on the "suicide squad"—the special team that kicks off or receives the kickoff. Eventually, as time and injuries wear away the starting offensive and defensive platoons, he'll earn a place on one of them. A pro team is two teams, separate and distinct, with different coaches, different skills, different things to learn.

As the year winds down into December, he'll find he's no longer a rookie, except in name. His education as a pro is still far from complete; it will never be complete. In the season five or more years away when he finally leaves the sport, he will probably feel as many old pros feel, that he is quitting just as he is truly learning how to play football.

Interestingly, every pro football player must one day reinvent himself. His football career, by most standards, is quite short in years. He is vulnerable to injuries that may further threaten his longevity on the field of battle. Thus, he will go on in life—learning.

PRACTICE AND PLANNING

What happens for championship games shows the importance of continuous learning. On the same field where a particular game time will take place, players begin a meticulous preparation for the game. The stands are empty. The players, clad in sweat suits, begin the infinitely precise choreography of football, tracing plays over and over again. The field is a rehearsal area for an invasion, with the coaches translating their scouting reports into a plan of attack, then drilling the troops endlessly in the execution of the plan.

The coaching staff spends hours every day going over movies of the enemy in action, searching for a flaw in the defense or a telltale giveaway by an offensive player that may tip the defense to a play. "The biggest learning experience you have is the film," says former Washington Redskins Coach Joe Gibbs. "We're going to take everything we can from the films." From the hours of study come the strategies and tactics of this miniature warfare, and, finally, the staff decisions are translated into checks and circles on a blackboard and enshrined in the playbook, the shorthand of football.

THE JANUS FACE OF PUBLIC EDUCATION

The most important tools America has to get workers to think and work smarter and to succeed in the new economy are our schools. This fact of economic life is now widely shared public knowledge. Indeed, public education was injected into the 1996 presidential race as a high priority national concern. Americans witness the "whining" about school problems and partisan arguing about what to do.

The perception of a "crisis" in education places an unprecedented burden on American public education. It now faces a paradox aptly symbolized by an ancient Roman god of gates and doorways called Janus. The god was shown as having two faces looking in opposite directions. The situation for education is very Janus-like; it is presently seen as both the vital source of social and economic prowess and as a major cause of social and economic distress.

For proof, just consider these few typical comments from a long list of prominent leaders, both from within education as well as from outside.

- "If I've learned one thing, it's that the answer to virtually all our national problems – from international competitiveness to improving our standard of living to the very security of our nation – ultimately rests on one word . . . education." (Robert D. Kirkpatrick, Chairman, CIGNA)
- "The bottom line is, America's fight for long term competitiveness ultimately will be won or lost not in the halls of Congress . . . not in boardrooms around the world . . . but in America's classrooms." (John L. Clendenin, CEO, BellSouth Corporation Chairman, U.S. Chamber of Commerce)
- "American education is in trouble because the world around it has changed irrevocably while our schools have not. The demographic, economic, social, and cultural realities of the late 20th century require a new and different system of education." (Dennis P. Doyle, Senior Fellow at the Hudson Institute)
- "Ironically, at the very moment in history that our ideas are being embraced elsewhere, our own position is being weakened because of deficiencies in human capital. People may say ten or twenty years from now, 'The United States was the greatest democracy, the greatest military power, the greatest economic power in history, but by the end of the twentieth century it went into decline because Americans could not figure out how to fulfill their most basic obligation: how to raise and educate their children.' " (Bill Clinton)
- "The problems of schooling are of such crippling proportions that many schools may not survive. It is possible that our entire public education system is nearing collapse." (John I. Goodlad, *A Place Called School,* Director, Center for Educational Renewal, University of Washington)
- "The charge of mindlessness – of not thinking deeply about what we are doing in schools, sounded frequently over the last three decades, still echoes." (Theodore R. Sizer, Chairman, Education Department, Brown University)

The situation America's educators now find themselves in is captured well in the opening lines of A. A. Milne's *Winnie the Pooh*. Christopher Robin is dragging his stuffed bear, Winnie, down a flight of stairs by his foot. With every step, Winnie's head is banging against each stair. As this is happening, he is saying to himself, "If only my head would stop hurting for a while, then maybe I could figure out a better way of coming down the stairs."

We plan to help stop the hurt by suggesting better ways. We find that an in-depth understanding of the strategies and tactics of professional football offers practical solutions for dealing with needed school reforms and the restructuring of public education. The interaction with individuals is the essence of coaching, and that will never change. Further, since football is widely communicated and supported, the metaphor helps create a shared vision of both *what* should be done and *how* to do it.

In a *Sports Illustrated* article, Sally Jenkins (1991) writes about Billie Jean King, the tennis pro, one of only four athletes to make *Life* magazine's list of the 100 most important Americans of the 20th century. Her description reveals several important clues to the value added by an understanding of the sports metaphor.

> In her symbiotic, ordered view of the world, tennis is about fortitude—facing up to things—and the value of a good effort for its own sake. To her mind, the sport should be properly executed, pleasing to the eye and emotionally and intellectually gratifying.
>
> "It's about learning your craft," she says. "That's a wonderful thing—especially with today's consumerism and instant gratification. You can't buy that. It's about making decisions, corrections, choices. I don't think it's so much about becoming a tennis player. It's about becoming a person." (p. 72)

The American economy is in transition from an industrial economy to a knowledge economy. It calls for an intense focus on (1) ways to better understand the transformation, (2) how these changes should impact what we teach, to whom, and when, but especially, (3) how it is taught in our homes, schools, and workplaces.

Every day, we experience the unsettling effects of a massive shift away from the Industrial Age (Era 2), which dominated Western and European thought and economic trade since the mid-19th century. We have yet to come face-to-face with the *full force* of the Knowledge and Information Age.

During a major economic transition period, which may only come about every 60–80 years, the psychological and social turmoil we sense daily is more like the more gentle outer winds of a Class 5 Hurricane packing 150 mile per hour winds at its center. The change, now gradual but nonetheless certain, is bearing down upon us. It will dominate the 21st century.

THE CHANGING NATURE OF WEALTH

Wealth is defined in different ways in different economic eras. During the Agricultural Age (Era 1), people's wealth was determined by the amount of land they owned. In the Industrial Age (Era 2), the age most Americans know, ownership of factories, equipment, and energy to power them was the key. In the on-coming Knowledge and Information Era, wealth is determined by the optimal employment of human skill and intellect—*human capital.*

The importance of *physical capital* and *human capital* in each one of the three eras is unmistakable. In an agricultural economy, land is the physical capital; physical strength and endurance is the prime labor asset. In an industrial economy, what a corporation requires of its human capital (the men and women it employs) is a steady supply of relatively low-skill labor to use its physical capital (its machines and the energy to run them). In a knowledge and information economy, a high-performance company succeeds to the extent that its work force is composed of people who can think, use information, make decisions, and take responsibility for their own and company success (the pragmatic intellectual component of human capital).

Nations with the highest standard of living now compete based on their brains not their brawn or low skill. To still compete largely through brawn or low skill is to do so based on low wages—to compete with third-world countries. If we Americans do not want to get poor, we must compete by *getting smart.*

The Emerging Era

The higher wage workplace in America is changing. Companies that pay an attractive wage find fewer places to routinize work or to simplify required job knowledge. For example, in banking, increased use of technology has eliminated much of the routine, manual processing of work, once a principal feature of banking. Consolidation and subsequent downsizing of bank staffs attest to the change.

In the apparel industry, new production techniques have changed what workers are expected to do. New processes reward teamwork and the ability of individuals to cope with unpredictable problems without the need to call a supervisor.

Similar examples are seen every day in more and more product and service firms.

Companies facing fierce competition in a new global economy have already recognized the need to integrate traditionally separate functions—design, engineering, and marketing—then build flatter organizations to decentralize responsibility and place greater emphasis on worker involvement at all decision making and problem solving levels.

An observer of the fading Industrial Age would summarize the changes this way:

(*1*) The number of well paying lower-skill jobs is declining.

(*2*) The need for increased skills and knowledge for higher paying jobs has grown.

(*3*) The long-term value of any current stock of knowledge steadily declines.

(*4*) The need to learn how-to-learn and continuous learning is job one priority.

The current transformation marks its beginnings in the mid-1950s. Ironically, it started at the height of American industrial power when, to all outward appearances, the U.S. showed evidence of being the world's preeminent representative of the Industrial Age.

In retrospect, the pace of the 1950s seemed quite slow. But it was during this post World War II decade that the birth-control pill came about, television came into almost every home, eager veterans came out of college with degrees financed by the "GI bill," and security meant finding a good white-collar job. The baby boom was in full flourish, and promise of the good life was just around the corner after 4 years of wearing a military uniform. David Halberstam (1993) in his book *The Fifties* relates, "In the years following the traumatic experience of the Depression and World War II, the American Dream was to exercise personal freedom not in social and political terms, but in economic ones" (Preface, p. x).

Overlooked was the approaching end of the era marked by the dominance of blue-collar work. By 1956, for the first time in American history, white-collar workers in technical, managerial, and clerical jobs—positions directly involved in the process and distribution of information—outnumbered blue-collar workers.

Today's marriage of technologies did not bring about the new information society. It has come about in response to global economic change. And with it, the time units of change have now moved from decades to single years.

Throughout the 20th century, the Industrial Age is all we have known. It has molded our economic and trade policies. It continues to dramatically affect our schools, our learning, and our view of the world. It has left us stuck on a slippery slope.

Change is no stranger to American life. Americans have long been change-prone. We are a change-accepting people. Consider what might be called ordinary American change from the perspective of even the first half-decade of the 20th century.

In the biography of Harry Truman (McCullough, 1992), we get a graphic picture of ordinary American change in a portrait of events the President's mother experienced during her lifetime.

> Martha Ellen Young Truman had been born in 1852 when Millard Fillmore was President, when Abraham Lincoln was still a circuit lawyer in Illinois, when her idolized Robert E. Lee was superintendent of West Point overseeing the education of young men from both the North and South. She had seen wagon trains coming and going on the Santa Fe Trail. She had been through civil war, survived Order No. 11, survived grasshopper plagues, flood, drought, the failures and death of her husband, the Great Depression, eviction from her own home. She had lived to see the advent of the telephone, electric light, the automobile, the airplane, radio, movies, television, short skirts, world wars, and her adored eldest son sitting at his desk in the White House as President of the United States. (p. 571)

Aside from having a son become President, this was a rather typical story for a surprising number of Americans.

Sports as Metaphor

One of the most powerful tools to help us perceive and then act wisely in this societal and economic transition comes from the world of sports. Sporting events are always in motion—constant change—even if one team calls "time out." Disciplined mind-body training, individual and team coaching and teaching, organizational success, and fan satisfaction serve as models for dealing with the needed change.

The sports metaphor helps us uncover several missing, neglected, and ignored paradigms (models of thinking). They will be of particular value in helping you develop and revise your own playbook for contending with the educational and economic shocks on their way from this transition.

Insights and best practices of team sports, especially professional football, can help our schools face the profound questions about the nature of education and how people learn. Through the sports metaphor, we find out what's needed to help build a playbook for practical and constructive change.

First, we have filed some pre-game scouting reports, giving the reader critical intelligence from the outside, from some thoughtful clients and "customers." These reports often contain critical comments and judgments, but they also contain gems of wisdom and practical suggestions.

The authors have the experience and skill to make discriminating judgments and evaluations about which of these factors are most valid as well as potentially most helpful for developing a playbook for successful performance when game time arrives in the new season, as it does each fall in U.S. school systems.

Building your playbook – preparing for the global economic game – has application for educators and stakeholders in three distinct areas:

(*1*) Policy development and policy engineering

(*2*) Process implementation in schools and colleges

(*3*) Economic advantage, personally and with community and the nation

Table 1.1 summarizes the paradigms used throughout the book.

Things to Remember

There are five critically important things to remember about the shift in context from an industrial-based national economy to an electronically driven, knowledge and information-saturated, world economy:

(*1*) We now live in a world of *interdependent* communities

(*2*) Interdependent communities are at the same time competitors and collaborators (we call this phenomena *coopetition*)

(*3*) Human capital (e.g., skilled, educated people) is central in the global transformation

(*4*) Continuous improvement of human capital through guided learning experience is the key to competitive superiority (we show this to be an *American kaizen*)

(*5*) Enterprises most likely to meet the demands of the changing

Table 1.1. *Era 2/Era 3 Transition Perspective.*

Sports—NFL Football	Think and Work Smarter
Training, practice, coaching, scrimmage, farm system, from Pop Warner league to the pros.	Developing and applying unique forms of continuous improvement.
Plays, moves, equipment, game strategies, tactics, practice sessions.	Mind Tools—Unlearning the most disabling paradigms; those outdated mental models.
The game remains in motion. Opposition is always changing. Every event is a new one.	Learn to see, think, and act from various points of view—quickly.
The number one play in sports is marketing. It is all geared around the fan.	Deliver maximum customer satisfaction. This is the only game in town.
Organized leagues, teams, free agents, rules help assure economic success.	Cooperate and compete at the same time with the same parties—global or local.
Scouting, benchmarking, analyzing game performance, a learning enterprise.	Learning communities/companies—adapting new realities to a new campus.

economic context act to become learning companies (part of *the learning commonwealth*).

Lester Thurow, Professor of Management at MIT, in his book *The Future of Capitalism* (1996) gives us two frameworks for capturing the meaning of this contextual shift: *plate tectonics* from geology and *punctuated equilibrium* from biology.

> In geology the visible earthquakes and volcanoes are caused by the invisible movement of the continental plates floating on the earth's molten inner core. . . . Corporate downsizings rock human foundations (expectations about their economic futures) as profoundly as any earthquake. (p. 6)

> Normally evolution proceeds at a pace so slow that it is not noticeable on a human time scale. . . . But occasionally something occurs that biologists know as "punctuated equilibrium." The environment suddenly changes and what has been the dominant species rapidly dies out to be replaced by some other species. (p. 7)

Putting the Focus on Schools

Schools are the focus of attention because there is considerable evidence that we can do something constructive about them. Schools are creatures of government As citizens in a democracy, we have a political "tool kit," a potentially powerful set of methods and mindsets that often results in improvement. We refer to the elected officials (governors, mayors, congressmen, state legislators, school board members); the statutes, rules, regulations, and dollars spent and withheld; and, in the final analysis, the major tool in a democracy, the capacity to shape attitudes and mobilize public opinion—something we hope this book will assist in doing.

Schools bear the brunt of concern because they are the most important institution and potential influence, after the family, in the lives of children and their future in the workplace. It is to be expected that heavier burdens are placed on the schools.

There is a direct relationship between learning and earning. Learning is the *ration card* to entry and sharing in a higher living standard. Rationing, unknown to younger Americans, is familiar enough to readers who recall World War II. During the war, many essential goods were scarce. The war effort took priority for raw materials, foodstuffs, oil products, and other essentials. Scarcity brings inflation. As a means of holding price levels in check and for a fair way of distributing essential goods to people, each American family and business was issued ration cards to allocate access to scarce necessities, such as sugar, gasoline, and tires.

A 1973 Middle East oil crisis forced Americans to once again experience the basic lessons of scarcity, elevated prices, and distribution. A rationing system was quickly put in place to equitably allocate limited supplies of gasoline. It was not uncommon to sit in your car for an hour or more in line just to receive 10 gallons of gasoline.

In a knowledge economy, driven by cognitive processing of information, learning is the rationing system that will help open the gates to new chances for gaining a higher share of wealth. The new relationship between factors of production—physical capital, financial capital, and human capital—show

- *human capital* (knowledge and skills) becomes the basic energy to drive the other factors of production
- knowledge and skill is the new form of capital accumulation

Learning—schools and continuous learning—determine one's access to chances for gaining wealth and a potential proportionate share of a higher standard of living.

This point was graphically driven home by the principal of Denver's North High School, an inner-city school. The school, with the city's highest drop-out rate, introduced a new weapon to get kids to "think" before quitting: a "Certificate of Dropping Out."

Each student must sign a disclaimer acknowledging that "I realize that I will not have the necessary skills to survive in the 21st century." Principal Joe Sandoval presented the disclaimer to two students—who both changed their minds. "It's like a brick went down their throat when they realized the consequences of their decisions," said the principal. Students who want to drop out must also bring their parents to a conference.

This is powerful stuff. But our question is more fundamental: "Can our schools assure those students who remain in school that they will have the necessary skills to survive in the 21st century?" We think they can. Some already do.

> To be fully effective in achieving potential productivity improvements, technological innovations also require a considerable amount of human investment on the part of workers who have to deal with these devices on a day-to-day basis. On this score, we still may not have progressed very far. Many workers still possess only rudimentary skills in manipulating advanced information technology. In these circumstances, firms and employees alike need to recognize that obtaining the potential rewards of the new technologies in the years ahead will require a renewed commitment to effective education and training, especially on-the-job training. This is especially the case *if we are to prevent the disruptions to lives* and the nation's capacity to produce that arise *from mismatches between jobs and workers.* We need to improve the preparation for the job market our schools do, but even better schools are unlikely to be able to provide adequate skills to support a lifetime of work. Indeed, *the need to ensure that our labor force has the ongoing education and training necessary to compete in an increasingly sophisticated world economy is a critical task for the years ahead.* (emphasis added)—Alan Greenspan, Chairman, Federal Reserve Board (Humphrey-Hawkins Testimony 2/20/96)

Clearly, higher levels of knowledge and skills are the new engines for creating new wealth as well as participation in the fruits of prosperity. And, it is in the partnering of schools and business, families and community that the engines are powered. Learning in Era 3 is the "royal road" to higher levels of earning.

AMERICAN *KAIZEN*

A powerful American legal framework brings us the concepts of *due care, due diligence,* and *due regard.* Derived from English common law and codified in part through tort law, it provides for the American economy what the Japanese cultural force called *kaizen* gives to that country.

The English translation of *kaizen* is *continuous improvement.* Business scholars uniformly attribute Japan's post-war "economics miracle" to their unique understanding, appreciation, and use of continuous improvement in their products and services.

Japanese continuous improvement led to Japan's success in the U.S. auto market, where today one out of three new cars sold either comes from Japan or is made in a U.S.-based plant owned and managed under Japanese quality standards.

In the post-World War II era, "Made in Japan" could best be described with such verbs as cheap, shoddy, inferior, shabby, flimsy, and poor quality. "Made in Japan" signified neither reliability nor customer focus. Price was the entry tool to the market, and share of the lucrative U.S. market was the goal. After more than 40 years, what we have now is revealed in the *Consumer Reports 1997 Annual Auto Issue:*

- The four most reliable new cars were Japanese.
- The seventeen best used cars were Japanese, the fifteen worst were American.
- Of the sixty-four cars receiving a CR check rating, thirty-eight were "Made in Japan," eighteen in the U.S.

There is a common law underpinning to our legal system. Its basis, if fully understood by the American people, is an American equivalent to Japanese *kaizen.* We draw from such common law principles as the "reasonable" person, the jury system, and the degrees of negligence to show how our notions of common sense can lead to continuous improvement of America's human capital.

A long line of famous American educators and business people, including Ben Franklin, Dale Carnegie, Horace Mann, Napoleon Hill, and Steven Covey, to name a few, have mined this depository of American common sense residing in common and tort law. The process we derive from this common sense cache, we call American *kaizen,* can successfully help us tackle education's most vexing problems, including how to optimize learning in schools, homes, and workplaces.

American *kaizen* fosters three essential elements for dealing with the demands of change in a time of fierce global competition: common sense, common virtues, and common goals. It is true as well that dealing with change comes down to the need (1) to unlearn old or bad habits, (2) to relearn the basics, the fundamentals of success, and (3) to learn what it takes to compete and prosper in a new global economy.

PRAXIS (WHAT WORKS) MAKES PERFECT

Every player of team sports instinctively knows the team cannot defeat its opponent without each player's mastery of essential requirements. The actions of precision thinking, strategy, and physical prowess of each individual player are indispensable parts of the "machine." Every player knows that all of the actions called for in the playbook are for naught if teammates fail in their individual tasks. You have to make the play when the ball is there. You've got to make it now.

In sports, especially professional football, we find specific ideas and techniques serve as a means of understanding and linking breakthrough and control with continuous improvement. These are the critical elements of practical and productive change.

Television, an early Era 3 device, has given untold thousands of sports fans the chance to watch action-packed football. The big plays, on-the-field antics, the color, and pageantry all add to the viewer's experience. Whenever it is game time, an NFL match-up is three things: sports, entertainment, and big business. Hidden from the fan's view are the great variety of factors at work among the players on the field, especially a team capable of consistently winning.

It is the mastery of many subtleties that helps mold world-class players—to learn how to quickly and positively adapt to a constantly changing battle. The winning player has an automated knowledge of fundamentals combined with superior physical and mental conditioning.

The top players always make "their practices" as the coach is fond of reminding them. Every successful athlete, irrespective of chosen sport, accepts the need to apply the processes of American *kaizen:* continuous learning, breakthrough, and control.

Consider the following elements of the sport:

- As a team, football players grind it out, yard by yard. Two yards, 3 yards, 5 yards—first down. Control and start again. Memorize your playbook.

- Each act illustrates the basic strategy for winning: *wear down your opponent.* Do more things right, and force the other guys to make more mistakes.
- In football, as in life, chance favors the better prepared (as Pasteur told us), plus a share of luck.

To quote a famous 20th century "sage," Groucho Marx, on football: "It's a common word, something you use every day." New things are hard to talk about; our experience moves much faster than does our language. In this respect, sports help us with multilayered ideas, such as continuous learning, personal development, and teamwork skills.

In sports, you have emotion, excitement, action. There is passion for the game. Players work against the clock. They make quick decisions and exchange quick communications. Because of its wide popularity, American culture has widely embraced and identified with the individual and team characteristics of football. For this reason, football, especially the NFL game, ably serves as a metaphor for playing and winning in the fast-changing global economic game. Thus, through the metaphor, we are able to enlarge our joint frame of reference.

LEARNING COMMONWEALTHS

Building learning communities highlights the new efforts to adapt schools, business, and government to the fast-changing new economic era. There is need for pragmatic action. Overcoming fear of change comes through the lens of corrective action.

Today, it is understandable that managers and educators find themselves tightly woven into an Era 2 fabric. Over these past many years, businesses and schools have built a closed system that has continued to insulate its members from outside pressures. Notwithstanding, it is important to keep in mind that it is at the outer boundaries of a system that there occurs a "bumping up" against the pressures of the outside world of change and chaos.

Today's fast-moving, information-rich, global economy exerts its pressures using a new set of demand drivers, each powered by customer satisfaction, a force-field that causes (or had better cause) reexamination of business practices, products, services, work force skills, and the performance of schools.

An Era 2 business manager or tenured educator is afraid of only two things. The first, if a new idea or method *does not* work, the manager or educator is anxious that he or she not be tagged with the blame for its failure and subsequently charged with fixing it, to correct it. The second, if a new idea *does* work, the manager or educator is fearful that he or she may be left embarrassingly standing at the gate for not having taken part in the successful effort to promulgate needed change.

In an entrenched bureaucracy, seemingly protected and not yet aware of an impending crisis, its strength lies in its ability to resist change, to maintain stability. Under such circumstances, it's easy to witness three common bureaucratic behaviors:

- They never admit they do not know.
- They never admit they are wrong.
- They never admit that others may know better.

Response then is predictable and painful. Business reacts by putting itself on a crash diet — right sizing, downsizing, restructuring — trying to transform itself into a new and more agile player.

Healthcare is a good example of what is yet to come. Starting in 1992 and in less than 3 years, the entire healthcare field has witnessed hospitals and doctors' offices transformed, forced by *the paying customer* — the patient backed by large employers and their insurance carriers who have demanded lower per-unit healthcare costs, greater accountability, and measurable healthcare outcomes. More than half of all U.S. doctors today work in an HMO-type practice.

Similarly, an impending storm, collapse, and restructure is headed toward education. From the colleges and universities to the secondary and elementary schools, educators are engaging in some form of change, seeking ways to deliver cost-effective user-satisfactory results.

Our intention is not to change the goals of schools and business, just to change the *methods* to reach the goals. And, for those who already recognize actions needed to facilitate change, to help focus on methods most likely to yield effective results.

LEADERSHIP

Work force development points to a game driven by fast-moving information and being played on a global ball field. Success requires a focus on building a playbook for breakthrough, control, continuous improvement, and scoring.

The school-to-work collaboration within the community overcomes the tunnel vision still held by many local government officials who still believe that they can revive our older urban areas or control suburban sprawl while ignoring the factor that is most relevant to a family's choice of where to live—the public schools.

It is a well-known fact that in school districts around the country, urban neighborhoods are routinely avoided by young families who can afford to live elsewhere. Meanwhile, the schools seem to worsen, because only those residents who lack other options are forced to send their children there. Simply stated, no family who has a choice would allow their children to attend a school where students are merely implored not to drop out, rather than one where students are challenged to learn and excel.

Many businesses and schools remain mired in the Era 2 mindset, outdated processes, management methods, and bureaucracy. Unchanged, the people involved can expect to remain under siege from the challenges of Era 3.

Taking the field of battle in such uncertain times against well-entrenched structures and ideas calls for selective actions. It is necessary to know which skirmishes to join and which skirmishes to avoid. Schools and teaching must deliver cost-effective results geared to the new realities, or both are destined to perish as we presently know them.

PRAGMATISM IS THE KEY

The spirit of this effort resides in its pragmatic orientation. America is the "can do" nation. Recall the slogan of our military? "The difficult we do immediately, the impossible takes a little bit longer." In NFL football, "Winners do what they have to do to win."

If the modern American reality is that parents work, then schools must deal with that. An answer? Extended-day programs, supervised homework, and enriched after-school programs offer a few, or at least the start of solutions.

If untold numbers of students enter school malnourished, abused, and using drugs, what is to be done? Teachers must receive training in social work and must have the required logistical support in order to recognize a troubled child and take appropriate measures.

If the "agrarian" calendar no longer suits the realities of American cultural and economic life, schools must consider major structural and organizational changes.

If nearly two-thirds of women with children work outside the home, then an extended school day or school-based day-care is needed.

If the world of work measures people's performance, then a performance-based, rather than a time-based, curriculum is needed.

The playbook series identifies and will help foster what works—the praxis that makes perfect.

CHAPTER 2

Game Time in Business: Understanding America's Transition Era

> "This is a football . . . a prolate spheroid—that is, an elongated sphere in which the outer leather casing is drawn tightly over a somewhat smaller rubber tubing. Better to have died a small boy than to fumble this ball."—Coach John William Heisman, namesake of the Heisman Trophy, college football's highest honor

AT ONE TIME, a student could look across the classroom at someone he or she would one day compete with for a job. In a global economy, he or she now competes for economic survival with students schooled in Asia, Latin America, or Europe, and other parts of the globe. More than ever, there is now an iron link between what we know and can learn and how well we can earn our daily bread.

America's education system must increase the percentage of young people entering the work force with *new economy skills*; and the majority of the present work force will need to "rethink" and "retool" their skills, to hold our own in the global economy.

The emerging information-rich economy has created a new pattern of jobs while, at the same time, made obsolete many job categories. There is evidence of the need for more highly skilled, but fewer production workers; fewer middle managers, more electronic information workers; and increasing numbers of "smart worker teams." Bulletin 2472 titled *Employment Outlook: 1994–2005: Job Quality and Other Aspects of Projected Employment Growth*, published by the U.S. Bureau of Labor Statistics said

- Occupations that will have the highest percentage growth are tied to health, computers, electronics, counseling, records technicians—all jobs requiring highly knowledgeable and skilled workers.
- Jobs requiring an associate degree from a community college will grow faster than average. Jobs for those with a master's degree from a college will grow the most, almost 28 percent.
- A bachelor's degree or more will be required in nearly 6 million new jobs.
- High-paying jobs will grow faster than low-paying jobs. Sixty percent of new jobs will offer above-average wages.
- Almost one million additional people are expected to join the ranks of the self-employed.

> In the Era 2 economy, capital meant bank accounts, shares of stock, assembly lines, and physical assets. In the Era 3 economy, human capital means the skill, talent, knowledge, and commitment of people and their optimal use on the job.

GLOBAL ECONOMIC PERSPECTIVE

Opponents of full U.S. participation in the global economy often try promoting fear. They cite loss of jobs, empty factories, bread and soup lines circa 1929. On the other hand, supporters of the new form of vigorous competition look forward to the challenge of the global economy with the confidence and with the judgment that the U.S. can not only regain the lead in the global economy but also go on to help shape its future.

There will be consequences if we fully proceed into the new economy. There will be consequences if we fail to proceed. The message will either be that America is ready for the 21st century or that America has lost its vision and will to compete. This is the kind of choice that confronts us today. It will have an impact on generations to come; it will send a clear message to our neighbors in the global village.

Active participation in the new global economy is not a one shot deal; it is not a single decision made at one point in history. It is a gradual process, with pivotal choices made years or even decades apart. Si-

multaneous international cooperation and zealous competitive participation in the global economy is our best, and perhaps only, hope for
creating world-class paying jobs for Americans. Investing in the future
can come about by creating the highest skilled, best trained, and most
productive work force in the world.

LEARNING—THE RATIONING HAND OF WEALTH CREATION

More than ever before, learning has become the rationing hand that
distributes financial rewards and security in the American economy.
America's capacity to mount an armada of workers with upgraded
knowledge and thinking skills adds up to this nation's intellectual capital. The promise for strengthening, rebuilding, and growing the U.S.
economy is in the total amount of effective national thinking skill we
can put on the global playing field.

Financial borders are not guarded walls. They are more like bridges
encouraging cooperation and partnerships. In a complex, information-
rich, global economy, no nation can afford to "go it alone," because
each is now part of an interdependent financial whole.

America's new mission in the new global economy is to find opportunities to lead and to engage in ventures with enterprises of different
nations. There are many examples to follow: Ford Motor Company
(U.S.) and Mazda Motors (Japan) set a standard for coopetition
(competition and cooperation at the same time with the same
party)—the collaborative design and manufacturing of branded auto-
mobiles and trucks, and then vigorous competition for vehicle sales
and leasing; Isuzu builds sport utility vehicles and trucks for Honda
and its luxury division Acura; Mitsubishi Motors and Chrysler did
joint designs and made sports cars for Dodge; Nissan builds mini-vans
for Mercury. IBM, Apple, and Motorola jointly developed a high-
powered processor chip, then later each built separate computer products. Daewoo (S. Korea) for several years built the Pontiac LeMans
(U.S.), which is marketed by General Motors against Hyundai (S.
Korea).

The European Community (EC) formed its common market and currency. Now NAFTA (North American Free Trade Alliance) has
spawned a free-trade North American continent, where tri-nation en-

terprises and workers will at times cooperate and at other times compete. And SEATA (South East Asian Trade Alliance) is being formulated into a regional trading bloc in response to EC and NAFTA.

Fast moving changes in regional and global business relationships eventually come around to affect every American worker. No longer can a manager count on the status quo to plan ahead. New products and multiple plant locations affect manufacturing planning. In turn, each worker needs to view these global dynamics and changes as a whole new ball game. What holds back the worker from fast, adaptive change is once again illuminated brightly by the football metaphor.

TODAY'S PLAYER IS DIFFERENT

Let's look at it through the prism of change in the world of sports. Until the late 1960s, athletes were developed in a very regimented and highly disciplined manner. The crew haircut (short, flat-top, military style) was in. Training habits, sleep, no smoking, no booze helped concentrate the player's mind on health and fitness for the game. Coaching staffs were given a high degree of respect, routinely called mister, and rapid motivation was the norm. Coaches worked within a pretty well accepted set of guidelines, and players knew and accepted exactly what was expected of them at all times.

Then came the turbulent days of the likes of N.Y. Jets star quarterback "bad boy" Joe Namath who both played hard (on and off the field) and was very outspoken. This behavior directly impacted the traditional way of coaching—and playing.

"I'm a pretty confident guy," Namath said in an interview. "I know what my abilities are. I know that if you add up all the things a quarterback needs—the ability to throw, to read defenses, to call plays, to lead the team—nobody has ever played the quarterback position any better than I do." In response to another reporter's questions, he said, "Sure I think I can win. In fact, I absolutely guarantee it."

Super Bowl III made Namath a national celebrity. In the biggest pro game of his career, Namath completed seventeen of twenty-eight passes for 206 yards and was named most valuable player (MVP).

For the first time in the history of football, a new kind of ball player emerged. "Now the game is more personalized—coach and player know each other by their first name," notes former San Francisco 49ers

Coach Bill Walsh. Athletes began to question authority. "Players ask more questions, especially the why questions," said former Miami Dolphins Coach Don Shula.

They wanted to know *why* a particular excrcise or drill had to be carried out and *why* training rules had to be adhered to. Much the same as educators and employers had experienced with students and workers, it became a time when football coaches had to learn and change to accept the new reality or become ineffective.

This all reads like ancient history now. A whole new generation of players has grown up since, yet some coaches (as well as teachers and business managers) continue to lament that ball players aren't the same as they used to be. Typical complaints include

- Players just aren't hungry enough these days.
- Players just aren't as competitive as their fathers used to be.
- Today, if a player finds he's not a star, he just up and quits trying.

Remember, these are not the excuses of the players; they are the opinions being expressed by coaches (as well as teachers and managers). That's the critical difference, because it's not so much that the ball players have changed with the times but rather it's sometimes the individual coach who has been unable to keep up.

Back when the authors were playing ball, players never questioned the coach, never thought of ever giving up on anything, and always gave it their all. What motivated us when we played ball doesn't necessarily motivate ball players today. If we can remember and grasp this basic bit of applied psychology, coaches (and teachers and managers) can save themselves a whole lot of frustration when trying to motivate their players (or students and workers) and the team.

Today, there is a psychology of winning: high energy, be enthusiastic, make it different all the time. Communications is the key. Keep it lively. Keep their attention.

IMPORTANCE OF THE KNOWLEDGE WORKER

The Industrial Age began when machines could replace muscle power. In the transition to the Knowledge and Information Age, machines supplement brainpower. Heavy manufacturing in such areas as steel, autos, rubber, and textiles is now impacted by knowledge intensive technology, while newer industries such as aerospace, computers, telecommunications, home electronics, pharmaceuticals, and health services using new technologies have grown even larger.

In the two decades between 1970 and 1990, approximately 90 percent of the new jobs created in the United States took place in the information processing and knowledge services areas such as finance, broadcasting, healthcare, education, law, accounting, data processing, and entertainment. The *infotainment* industry is now estimated to be a one *trillion* dollar industry annually.

As more jobs come from information and knowledge services, the information worker (popularly called the white-collar worker) increases his or her share of the total work force. If to this we add the *gold-collar* worker – college-educated professionals such as lawyers, doctors, security analysts, consultants, accountants, engineers, computer programmers, and college professors, whose work centers around applying knowledge to problem solving – the nature of the work force shift becomes even clearer.

Studies from the U.S. Department of Education in 1996 show the positive correlation between education and livelihood. College graduates make more money than high school graduates. The supporting details are dramatic: workers with a college degree had average monthly salaries of $2,339. Those with some college but no degree averaged $1,303; those with only a high school diploma made $1,080 monthly. And if the worker didn't complete high school, the wages averaged only $508 a month.

The conclusion is inescapable: *in most cases* the more formal education one has, the more money one can make. Conversely, those with little formal education are practically doomed to economic adversity. Education is not only society's ration card for sharing wealth, it is also the catalyst for creating new wealth. In the transition to a new economy, we have entered the *Era of Human Capital*, a period in which talent, intelligence, and knowledge are the basic components for world-class economic prowess.

A GLOBAL ECONOMIC MINDSET

Workers in the developing nations of Southeast Asia, India, Mexico, and Eastern Europe are portrayed as poor and underpaid, producing goods for global export, many of which are imported into the U.S. Many NAFTA arguments centered on whether Mexican citizens could even afford U.S. export goods.

In *Business Week* (October 25, 1993), "Selling to the New Global Middle Class," offered startling facts on the new and emerging global markets. According to *Business Week*, there are some 400 million members of the new global middle class; about 100 million of them are ex-communist-country residents, formerly trapped behind the iron curtain. Another 300 million are graduates of what was once considered "merely" third-world countries.

Added to an already large and established middle class in Western Europe, the magnitude of this unprecedented global economic trading opportunity is just beginning to hit home. America's corporate trading history has been built around "the market-oriented, capitalist-trading system composed of North America, Europe, and Japan." In recent years, S.E. Asia, China, Eastern Europe, Russia, and Latin America have all "gone market." Even India, with a high middle class, is in the process of opening its markets to the global economy. "The total for people participating in the open global market? Three billion and counting," writes *Business Week*.

Another revelation to American workers and employers is the extent to which their worldwide counterparts are becoming more prosperous. It's estimated that 10 percent of China's 1.2 billion people (that's 120 million or almost half the size of the total U.S. population) can now own their own homes and have a TV set. Nearly half the people in South Korea, Taiwan, Hong Kong, and Singapore have reached the coveted rung on the middle class ladder. In Thailand, Malaysia, and Indonesia "up to 20 percent of the population is headed there too. And tens of millions more in Mexico, Chile, and Argentina, soon to be joined by people from Eastern Europe, Russia, and the Mid-East."

South Korea is a fast growing market. While having only 45 million people, its consumer purchasing power is much greater than China's—over $10,000 per capita. American companies like Estee Lauder and Clinique cosmetics, Whirlpool refrigerators, and Levi Strauss jeans are there to serve the high-end market. And Ford is building their Southeast Asia franchise as one of the top selling "imported" luxury auto brands.

American workers and businesses continue focusing on our negative balance of trade and the stream of goods flowing into the U.S. Its impact on domestic competition—holding down wages and cutting jobs — is a major concern. It is a principal focus of the playbook for the new global economy. We seek to persuade educators to revamp their Industrial Age thinking and now help America's workers and employers seize the leadership of a 21st century economic renaissance.

BENCHMARK: OPHELIMITY AS CUSTOMER FOCUSED QUALITY

The U.S. and 116 other nations agreed to substantially reduce tariffs and to revise the framework that has governed most international trade since World War II. The accord, the General Agreement on Tariffs and Trade (GATT), is expected to only modestly stimulate global business and investment activity by opening markets and encouraging countries to specialize in producing whatever goods they can make most efficiently — the traditional rule of comparative advantage. By itself, its effect on America's economic growth is expected to be marginal.

The Knowledge and Information Era mindset, centered in the concept of ophelimity, is to business and education what the obsession with satisfying fans is to professional football. What follows shows why.

It's been almost half a century since J. M. Juran published the first *Quality Control Handbook* (1951). It made available, in ready reference form, principles and practices for achieving better quality in producing products and services at lower cost. Between its covers were references to the work of Bell Labs' Dr. W. A. Shewhart and W. Edwards Deming, who had demonstrated the statistical relationships between quality control and productivity. Together, Juran, Shewhart, and Deming fostered Total Quality Management (TQM), the leading candidate as the quintessential process for the emerging Information Age economy.

Quality is a complex concept. In the new economy, there is a growing consensus about its definition. Quality in the new global economy is best defined as fitness for customer use (variety, customization, convenience, timeliness, exemplary service) as judged by the user — the customer or client.

Ophelimity is a word poised for oblivion. We need it now to describe an economic survival concept, though it may not appear in most dictionaries. *Webster's Third International New Dictionary* still has it: "Ophelimity: useful, helpful, economic satisfaction." So does *Oxford's:*

"Ophelimity: the ability to satisfy any want . . . the relationship of convenience which makes a thing satisfy a need or want."

Juran, in the *Quality Control Handbook,* discusses the concept. It appears in the fundamental definition of quality as fitness for use.

> It would be most desirable to agree upon a single short phrase to designate fitness for use in all situations. The word "system" is too elaborate for the bulk of the concerns, e.g., food, clothing, shelter. The word "product" fails to include the service industries. Serious consideration should be given to a word not in common use, so as to avoid the reflexes and vested interests associated with words already in use.
>
> An interesting nomination is the word "ophelimity." The literal meaning is "power to give satisfaction," with a connotation that economic satisfaction is involved. The word is derived from the Greek "ophelimos," which means helpful, useful. (p. 2–3)

Consistent with the history of quality and current dictionary meanings, we define ophelimity as "the power to give customer satisfaction." Given this meaning, the word provides a unique match with the total quality element of the new economy—a customer-centered process. Like professional football's passion for satisfying, even dazzling, its fans, Era 3 enterprises must have the same mindset to gain and keep customers.

Ophelimity is also the quality benchmark of an Era 3 enterprise. It is the single most reliable contributor to output in the 21st century global economy, because in the final analysis, only the user makes the final judgment on a product or service and its fitness for use. This goes doubly for consumers of different cultures.

ERA 3 AMERICAN BUSINESS EXAMPLES

Helios, a new medical imaging system from Polaroid Corporation, reached the market after just 3 years of R&D. That was twice as fast as even the most aggressive optimists at Polaroid had predicted. Company leaders gave as the reason for the speed and timeliness of the market introduction the interdisciplinary teamwork in their labs. "Our researchers are not any smarter than those of our competitors," the CEO stated, "but by working together through *shared mental models* they get the value of each other's intelligence almost instantaneously."

At Pioneer Hi-Bred International, scientists breed several strains of corn for disease resistance, high yield, or for specific attributes like oil content. A decade ago, such work required hundreds of farmland acres and consumed myriad costly work hours. Currently, the company can do it by directly manipulating the plant's DNA using a petri dish. Aside from cost savings, the essential productivity component, the company trimmed 2 years off the 7- to 10-year time cycle ordinarily needed to develop a new hybrid and bring it to market.

IDS Financial Services, the financial planning subsidiary of American Express Company, codified the expertise of its best account managers in a software program called *Insight*. Now the least able of their 6,500 financial planners is better than an average planner used to be. One powerful outcome: In 4 years, the percentage turnover of IDS clients was cut by 50 percent.

Unfortunately, many American organizations still apply mid-20th century thinking to 21st century challenges. They are not following the pioneering path of the examples described above.

The obstacle is one of mindsets, not methods; the problem is cognitive, not cosmetic. As in football, when you "come off the line" with playbook assumptions drawn from out-of-date game films that no longer fit a changed reality, it's hard to gain any new yardage.

> "Great players cause you to change your strategies."—Joe Gibbs, Washington Redskins

In the business world, post World War II American management thinking got stuck on standardization, production efficiency, and cost control as the driving values to support profit goals. It placed its highest value on quarterly financial results, numbers that, in part, are driven by accounting policies and the equity markets. It also saw in advertising the major tool to promote standard products, and with it, manufacturing efficiencies, overhead absorption, and lower output costs. It turned to advertising, not better quality, as its road to success.

On the other hand, successful foreign competition departed from such tunnel vision thinking. It turned adroitly toward quality as the driving value for profit. It targeted increased market-share and long-term customer relationships as having the highest value. It viewed step-by-step improvement as creating the winning appeal of product and/or service to the customer.

In the global economy, successful American companies increasingly accept that quality is the key to both productivity and competitiveness. They know that quality builds upon people skills and the company's ability to use highly skilled people to maximum workplace advantage. Successful companies have already begun shifting their paradigm (mental model) to match the terms and conditions of a cognitive global economy.

For much of the 20th century, American enterprise has been organized on the principle that most of us *do not* need to know much to do the work that has to be done. The information-rich, global economy is organized on the principle that most of us *do* need to know much to do the work that has to be done.

AN ERA 3 PARADOX: MORE COMPETITION MEANS MORE COOPERATION—COOPETITION

More competitors and competitors' products demand increased flexibility and quick response. These circumstances require five forms of partnership:

- between enterprises and often sole source suppliers, especially education
- between enterprises needing to mutually prosper on a global playing field
- between workers to speed action where it counts—with the customer
- between management and the work force
- between an enterprise and its distributors, franchisees, and representatives

To effectively compete, we must learn to cooperate with all sets of partners, many of whom are new to our historical experience. It means extensive use of electronic linkup—getting closer to the customer with programs, resources, and services. It concerns computer-integrated manufacturing (CIM) and flexible manufacturing systems. It is at least as much about forming partnerships among functions within the enterprise as with suppliers, distributors, sales reps, and, ultimately customers.

Adversarial relations in areas such as these have been characteristic of most firms in the past. Today, they spell competitive discomfort and doom chances for success tomorrow.

Coopetition—simultaneous cooperation and competition—reveals a new model of global economic activity. Its benefits:

- It buffers some of the negative impacts of change.
- It helps speed up conversion to the new economic structure that can move swiftly and surely on the information-rich, global playing field.
- It saves time by reducing the steep learning curve associated with key business functions (production and marketing) in a culturally diverse new venture.

Teamed with the American model of what the Japanese call *kaizen,* the forces of education and learning could be deployed to turn enterprise and workers into world-class performers.

Changes in the economy have gradually spawned the horizontal organization where workers and managers concentrate on satisfying customer needs based on user standards, not on hierarchical position. GE and AT&T, DuPont and Boeing, among others, have flattened their organizations to gain speed and flexibility unmatched by the traditional power structure.

Real horizontal enterprises go further than redrawing the organization chart, however. They arrange workers into self-managing teams. Such teams have fundamentally changed all roles and responsibilities — and compensation. Lower-level workers are asked to take on more responsibilities for broader issues. Senior managers give up some control. These changes represent nothing less than a revolution in corporate culture.

The shift to the horizontal company in enterprises and schools also calls for a new structure for continuous learning. A 1996 Conference Board study showed "Action Learning" gaining momentum as a method in training managers. "It's real basic stuff, but it works," said Gina Walters, a Conference Board research associate. Companies as diverse as McDonald's and Motorola identified global issues and competitive pressures as topping their list of major forces affecting management training.

No less than a complete transition of thinking and action will do, if the U.S. is to be a strong player in the global economy. And only a true understanding and use of American *kaizen* can help enterprises, workers, and schools hit the new moving targets—the 21st century economic and global objective.

Coopetition is more than a new approach to structuring international ventures. It is the 21st century way of tackling the global economic challenge of diverse markets, wide-area logistics, and broad cultural differences and defining our relationships with them.

FROM FLEXIBILITY TO IMMEDIACY

Change means opportunity as well as danger. In the same way that the Industrial Age wrought havoc on the land and farms of the Agricultural Age, the changes also led to expanding town and urban trading centers. With it came undreamed of prosperity as well as serious displacement of those unable to cope with the transition. No one can say for sure what new ways of working and prospering the forthcoming Information Age will bring with it. We already have some glimpses of what is about to overtake us. In a revolution, the only surety is surprise.

Today's enterprise is rapidly becoming a *just-in-time* enterprise: one that must adapt to continually changing stimuli coming from an information-driven, global economy. As more of the business system becomes paperless—for example, the electronic processing of a customer demand-to-order—delivery-to-invoice and receivable-to-cash will move at ever greater speed. The firm's critical agenda becomes that of converting operations and marketing from one of flexibility into immediacy.

Twenty years ago, everyone wanted to invent another Polaroid camera, have a comfortable little monopoly for 20 years, and make lots of money. In a fast moving economy where the typical lifespan of a consumer electronics product is between 2 and 3 months, the typical enterprise must now react to information immediacy.

The transition to this new, information-rich environment may be difficult. One economist put it wryly: "Adjustment is the dismal part of the dismal science." Or, as Robespierre observed on his way to the guillotine, "This time it's personal." The inescapable turmoil involves your enterprise, your career, and your quality of life.

For business, the message is loud and clear. New relationships in technology, marketing, manufacturing, and management often provide the decided edge. Knowing what the users value and providing it to them is the benchmark of quality. Using the principles of continuous learning and renewal is the mechanism for adaptive survival, individual and enterprise growth.

IN A TURNAROUND GAME, LEARNING IS
THE KEY FACTOR

No matter how it is measured by economists, education pops up as a major contributor to a country's economic growth. A recent RAND Corporation study "How Do Education and Training Affect a Country's Economic Performance?" brought to light that

- Regardless of the particular method used to measure its contribution, education and its effects on labor quality were among the most important contributors to a nation's economic growth.
- Countries with comparable levels of education are converging among themselves, but they are failing to close the economic gap with nations whose educational levels are higher.
- "Even economists who cannot be suspected of favoring any form of social policy acknowledge the importance of education and call for a higher priority on educational policy," concluded Ronald Sturm, the study author.

And a National Research Council study, "Charting a Course for Federal Post Secondary Policy," determined

- Individuals without a college degree stumble through a training system that is piecemeal and incoherent.
- They choose their own training, with little guidance, in a wide variety of settings, including community and technical colleges, vocational schools, and apprenticeship programs.

The report suggests that government act as catalyst to promote the development of a more coherent and effective system of training to tie eligibility for student aid to a vocational school's success in graduating and placing its trainees.

Many are experiencing the effects of the new economy directly in their workplace. In fact, today's workplace is no longer a "place" at all but more likely "an arena through which information circulates." The arena is not the kind of self-contained enclosure traditionally associated with the workplace. It is more likely defined by a question—a quest for knowledge—than by an organization chart or even a strategic plan. It is likely to be defined by a problem or process rather than a production or service plan.

SUDDENLY, A NEW BEGINNING

In his autobiography, General Colin Powell (retired) relates the experience of one day coming to grips with the fact that the Cold War was over. The U.S. game plan of containing communism had been swept away by a single pronouncement from then Soviet President Mikhail Gorbachev. Powell relates the event when, after leaning across a conference table and suddenly declaring an end to the Cold War, Gorbachev turned to him and said, "General, you will have to find yourself a new enemy."

Powell tells the story that with only a few years to go to retirement he thought to himself that the ground rules that had dictated the balance of power for the last 40 years, and his first 30 years of military service, had just gone out the window. With this change came the end of a bipolar world and the entire systems theory of how the world turns.

All at once, the free world more than doubled in size. New markets dramatically opened up. New opportunities for investment were available throughout the old iron curtain countries. The new global economy began shifting into higher gear.

To benefit from these changes, it was necessary to have more than merely access to information. What was needed was focused and dynamic information—even more so than capital. Overnight, the new currency of nations became brainpower.

> "The problem with most leaders today is they don't stand for anything. Leadership implies movement toward something, and convictions provide that direction. If you don't stand for something, you'll fall for anything."—Retired Miami Dolphins Coach Don Shula; from his autobiography *Everyone's a Coach* (1995)

It's fun to take a quick mental exercise before we close this section. In a knowledge-based economy, it would be nonsense to value the assets of Era 3 companies like America Online or Netscape or Microsoft as we would an Industrial Age company. When we ask these questions, the answers you give begin to help you build your playbook.

- How much land and buildings do they own? Does it really matter?
- How much inventory do they have on hand relative to brainpower?

- What is their office inventory? How much space do they need to think?
- What level of raw materials do they have on hand? Where in the world is it?

At Information Age companies, the assets walk out the door in the evening inside the heads of their workers. Many even leave in the morning after all-night sessions.

CHAPTER 3

Game Time in Education: Developing and Maintaining Human Capital

> It may seem paradoxical to interpret Henry Ford's importance in terms of a concept. . . . For he invented nothing, no new technique, no new machine, not even a gadget. What he supplied was *the idea of mass production itself:* organization of men, machines, and materials into one productive whole.—Peter Drucker (1971, p. 157)

AMERICA'S GREATEST ASSET is her people. Turning that fundamental axiom into educational practice is the key to preparedness for the 21st century.

Wealth has been defined in many different ways in the past. During Era 1, wealth was determined by land ownership. In Era 2, the key source of wealth was physical—factories, equipment, and energy to power them. All that corporations needed from their workers was a steady supply of low-wage help to operate under engineered supervision.

Here's the change. In the emerging Era 3, human capital is the key source of wealth. Around the globe, a highly competitive yet collaborative economy is burgeoning. And here is the bottom line: America, as a nation, will succeed only to the extent that every American can think and work smarter than, on average, Americans have ever done before. To do this, we must have a work force and citizenry who can think, use information, make informed decisions, and take individual responsibility. We can prosper economically by mastering the requirements of an *enriched cognitive economy.*

Developed nations currently meeting Era 3 requirements compete every hour based on their brains, not solely on their brawn. And any U.S. city, county, or state that still competes based on low wages and low taxes is competing with third-world countries; it competes based

45

on its willingness to have low-skilled U.S. workers do routine work at the same cost as workers in Mexico or Malaysia. The lure of cheap rural land, lower taxes, and the quality of non-urban life can only take us so far in the global game. If Americans don't want to get poorer, we must compete by *getting smart*. We cannot "muscle" or "over-power" our way to global economic success.

The most important settings we have to get smarter are in our homes, schools, and workplaces, in partnerships and alliances. Unfortunately, the institution supported by society to take the lead—public education—still prepares students for the Industrial Age.

PREPARING FOR THE LAST WAR

Historians have repeatedly documented the generals who have prepared for the last war. The French built the Maginot Line, a series of concrete bunkers along their common border with Germany to avoid a repeat of a World War I type invasion. In 1940, German tanks rolled around the line and conquered France in a matter of weeks. The U.S. Army Air Corps, prior to World War II, was not convinced of the power of aerial bombing until General Jimmy Doolittle took the bombs to Tokyo from an aircraft carrier. In Korea, American and South Korean troops moved north by truck and road, World War II style, while the North Korean forces moved southward through the jungles, never touching the roads. When General Matthew Ridgway got there, he put a stop to it. For 20 years, the French fought a jungle war in Vietnam with Legionnaires trained to fight in the African desert and as paratroopers. The Americans took over, moved into the jungle, and the enemy dug miles of underground tunnels to move their soldiers, like ants. Most recently, U.S. success in open desert warfare in Iraq left the generals totally unprepared for worldwide terrorist attacks against American military installations.

In the middle of this century, 60 percent of American jobs required little or no skills beyond a willingness to work hard and show up on time, attitudes still among the most basic requirements. Come the new millennium, that figure is projected to be under 15 percent. As a result, our schools must vastly increase the numbers of people prepared to succeed in the Era 3 economy.

Even the definition of what it means for the "average" person to be prepared is changing. Employers repeatedly tell us that they now need workers with knowledge and skills in elementary forms of logic, probability, and statistics; far more than the traditional high school content commonly taught in algebra, geometry, and trigonometry. Employers need workers who can read critically, think analytically, act creatively, communicate effectively, and work cooperatively with a diverse group of fellow employees. This is not the knowledge or the skills our schools or other formal training centers emphasize.

NEEDED: A NEW BASIC STATISTIC FOR AMERICAN SCHOOLING

The widening need to improve educational quality throughout the world has had many effects, none more far-reaching than the attention to costs and benefits. The question is basic: "How much does instruction cost, and what is the public getting for its money?"

Can the efficiency of use be measured? In terms of Era 3 requirements, a school cannot be said to operate efficiently and effectively if learning is not taking place. The playbook must apply a form of industrial product/service cost accounting to education.

Some may criticize looking at school as if it were a business. But, the real error lies in not using a business-like mindset. Educators have often failed to understand the significance of merely focusing on "lowest cost" independent of a direct linkage to "finest product." If they had focused additionally on quality, the results of applying a business mindset might have been more noteable.

Two major obstacles stand in the way of America producing our finest products in education. They come directly from (1) not specifying what our product is and (2) not clearly defining what we really mean by the finest or quality. In education, the basic statistic we use is *cost-per-student*. But, this indicator is not comparable to the cost-per-unit figures of industry—the difference being that industry identifies the cost-per-operable unit. The true cost of an industry's output includes not only each unit's intrinsic development cost but also the cost of those units that did not pass quality control, more specifically, scrap.

However, in education, we look typically at the cost-per-student-taught (input) and not the cost-per-student-learned (output). What is taught and what is learned are not synonymous. Unlike a business and

industry, educators have not been including the cost of our inade
quately prepared learners, students who cannot function in today's, let
alone tomorrow's, global economy to earn a decent living. We do not
arrive at the full cost of our education system. If we had, our actual
cost-per-student figures would be many times greater than the already
large amount expended relative to the rest of the world, now cited as
the national average.

We will improve education dramatically when we require educators
to calculate annually the *cost-per-prepared student;* the students who
have met the required standards to enter and compete on the world-
class, economic playing field. Attempts to reduce cost must be directed
at geometrically increasing the number of authoritatively prepared students.

AGREEMENT ON WHAT A *PREPARED STUDENT* MUST KNOW AND BE ABLE TO DO

In 1991, the Secretary of Labor and members of the Secretary's Commission on Achieving Necessary Skills (SCANS) published a set of
world-class work force standards. These people were concerned representatives of the nation's schools, businesses, unions, and government.
The standards reflected the result of their examining the major changes
in the world of work and the implications of those changes for learning.
Today, there is general agreement in state departments of education
throughout the nation that these standards should form the basic core
of learning for all students.

The commission members understood that schools do more than
simply prepare people to make a living. Thus, their report concerns
only one part of that education, the part that involves how schools prepare young people for work. It does not deal with other, equally important, concerns that are also the proper responsibility of our educators.

The report points out that for most of the 20th century, this nation
took its goods and know-how to the world. America scarcely needed to
worry about competition from abroad. At home, the technology of
mass production emphasized discipline to the assembly line. Today, the
report argues, the demands on business and workers are different.
Firms must now meet world-class standards and so must all workers.
Employers seek worker adaptability and their ability to learn and work
in teams.

This change has many implications. The focus first falls on the more than half of our young people who leave school without the knowledge or foundation required to find and hold a good job. The report sharply warns that unless *all* Americans work to turn this situation around, these young people, and their employers, will pay a very high price.

As they say around NASA, "this is rocket science"; but is the issue just about rocket science? Low skills lead to low wages and low profits. Many youth will never be able to earn a decent living. In the long run, it threatens the quality of life every American hopes to enjoy.

The Commission spent 12 months talking to business owners, to public employers, to the people who manage employees daily, to union officials, and to workers on-the-line and at their desks. They talked to them in their stores, shops, government offices, and manufacturing facilities. The message they heard was the same across the country and in every kind of job: good jobs depend on people who can put knowledge to work. New workers must be creative, responsible problem solvers and have the skills and attitudes on which employers can depend and build. Traditional jobs are changing, and new jobs are created every day. Higher paying but unskilled jobs are disappearing. Employers and employees share the belief that all workplaces must "work smarter."

From these conversations, three major conclusions came about:

(*1*) All American high school students must develop a new set of competencies and foundation skills if they are to enjoy a productive, full, and satisfying life. Whether they go next to work, apprenticeship, the armed services, or college, all young Americans should leave high school with the know-how they need to make their way in the world. In the SCANS report, know-how has two parts: (1) competence and (2) a foundation of skills and personal qualities. Less than one-half of our young people hold these. The report predicts that this know-how will be important to those who will be developing the world-class standards for educational performance.

(2) The report emphasizes that the qualities of high performance that today characterize our most competitive companies must become the standard for the vast majority of our companies, large and small, both local and global. By "high performance," they mean work settings relentlessly committed to excellence, product quality, and customer satisfaction.

(3) They declare that these goals are pursued by combining technology and people in new ways. Decisions must be made closer to the front line and draw upon the abilities of workers to think creatively and solve problems. Above all, these goals depend on people – on managers committed to high performance and to the growing competence of their work force; on responsible employees comfortable with technology and complex systems, skilled as members of teams, and with a passion for continuous learning.

The nation's schools must be transformed into high-performance organizations in their own right. Despite a decade of reform efforts, the findings of the report demonstrate little improvement in student achievement.

The reports says that we are not developing the full academic abilities of most students and are failing the majority of poor, disadvantaged, and minority youngsters. By transforming the nation's schools into high-performance organizations, we will have schools relentlessly committed to producing skilled graduates.

The report goes on to identify five competencies, that, in conjunction with a three-part foundation of skills and personal qualities, lie at the heart of job performance today. These eight areas represent essential preparation for all students, both those going directly to work and those planning further education. All eight must be an integral part of every young person's school life.

Seldom does one of these eight components stand alone in job performance. They are highly integrated, and most tasks require workers to draw on several of them.

The report has a serious message for employers as well as educators. Employers must orient their business practices to hiring and developing this know-how in employees. If they do not develop a world-class work force, the report argues that business inevitably will be at risk. Here is what they suggest *employers* can do.

- First, recognize your workplace must be in the high-performance environment of the future. Nine out of ten employers still operate on yesterday's workplace assumption. Do not be one of them.
- Second, invest in your employees so that they can obtain the skills needed to succeed in this new environment.
- Third, clearly tell educators what you need and work with them

to accomplish it. You know that students have to believe that you
care about what they learn.

* Employers who value performance in high school when they
  make their hiring decisions provide students with the right
  signal: learning and earnings are related activities.

Educators have to instill in students the perspective on results that the
SCANS skills demand. If they do not, they will be failing their students
and the community as they try to adjust to the 21st century. Speaking
directly to educators and imploring them to act, the SCANS report
states that they, more than anyone, are responsible for helping children
develop needed skills.

Here is how they argue educators can help:

* First, tell your students what the standards are—what is expected
  of them.
* Second, give them the benefit of a fair and firm assessment of
  where they stand and what they need to do. If they pass every
  grade and receive diplomas without mastering these skills, they
  cannot make their way in the world of work.
* Third, use the competencies and the foundation defined for
  every nook and cranny of the school curriculum. Your most
  gifted students need this know-how, as well as those
  experiencing the greatest difficulties in the classroom. If students
  are taught the know-how in the context of relevant problems, you
  will find them more attentive, more interested—indeed, more
  teachable—because they will find the coursework challenging
  and relevant.

The playbook addresses three fundamental challenges: (1) the demand for more knowledge and skills, (2) new knowledge and skills,
and (3) more broadly shared and distributed knowledge and skills.
Taken together, it will require enormous improvements in *what* we
teach, *when* it is taught, *to whom* it is taught, and *how* it is taught.

We need improvements in how we use what we know works to
achieve the required learning. Our learning centers, whether it be in
the home, in the school, or in the workplace, must teach more efficiently and more effectively. This is a basic economic necessity for the
nation. This means teaching new things along with the basics and
reaching populations long neglected or underserved.

BRINGING A NEW IDEA TO LIFE: AN AMERICAN MODEL OF JAPANESE *KAIZEN*

In our American legal framework, there exists a set of universal concepts and practices either unknown, neglected, or misunderstood by managers, educators, and the public, which, when properly applied, can help solve our present learning achievement problems in homes, schools, and workplaces. The framework comes from common law and tort law ideas such as due process, due diligence, and due regard. Taken together, it holds the potential to provide a powerful process for guiding learning, policy development and application, and for the personal caring so sorely needed for the continuous improvement of human performance.

At present, the framework is mandated by law as a protection of the employment rights for one class of public employees—public school teachers. Interestingly, the same mandated framework steps form the principles for the *guided learning experiences* that were successfully used to train virtually all the new and untried workers needed to produce the war material for World War II.

Properly employed, the framework provides a process for continuous development of human skill, knowledge, and attitude; the equivalent to what is known in Japan as *kaizen*—continuous improvement. We call the legally inspired framework American *kaizen*—America's cultural model for continuous improvement of human performance.

Widely understood and practiced to improve learning in our homes, schools, and workplaces, the framework can become America's leading "weapon" of economic advantage in today's fiercely competitive, yet collaborative, global economy.

Here, we unabashedly call upon the concept of American *kaizen* as the leading candidate to drive the "American economic miracle" in the emerging economic era of human capital. It has the potential to be our principal form of energy. What follows is a brief account of the American legal framework for guiding successful learning experience.

LEGAL FRAMEWORK FOR AMERICAN *KAIZEN*

In repeated court opinions, the concept of *substantive due process* in the common law is held to consist of five elements:

(*1*) Known expectations of what is required to be achieved

(*2*) Documented assistance in meeting the expectations

(*3*) Timely knowledge of results

(*4*) Feedback from the results to construct necessary corrective action

(*5*) Many changes to be successful through repetition of all the previous elements

Coach Vince Lombardi, then with the Washington Redskins, was one day baffled by the dull performance of Larry Brown, his 8th round draft pick. At 5′ 11″ and 195 pounds, he was a powerful running back. He had everything, including desire.

One evening while reviewing the game films from a pre-season exhibition game, Lombardi noticed something. He re-ran the film in slow motion. It became evident that Brown was a split-second later getting off the ball than his teammates. Lombardi asked Brown whether anything was wrong, and he replied with a stock answer used by rookies.

One day two men approached Brown in the locker room and asked him to leave the building. They had been ordered by Lombardi to give Brown a hearing test, which revealed that Brown was deaf in his right ear, something he had suspected since childhood, but never shared with anyone. When Lombardi got the diagnosis, he went to NFL Commissioner Pete Rozelle and obtained permission to have a hearing aid installed in Brown's helmet.

Coach Lombardi's ability to spot Brown's hearing problem saved the rookie's career. The next year, 1972, Brown won the NFL rushing title and was the unanimous choice for NFL Player of the Year.

Expectations, assistance, results, corrective action, and many chances are the "stuff" of *guided learning experience.* They are the fundamental elements of *due care.*

Due care consists of several mandated steps to assure that the rights to learn and therefore to succeed are protected. We define the due care component of American *kaizen* as *guided learning experience.*

To be faithful to the spirit of the common law mandate for substantive due process, the *guided learning experience* aspects must be energized by due diligence and due regard, two additional concepts from common law and codified in tort law:

* Due diligence is the requirement to be aware of problems and dangers *before* they become a pitfall. It mandates proactive intervention to prevent problems.

- Due regard embodies the required caring spirit of substantive due process — its soul. Its fundamental meaning is respect for every person with no strings, no requirements, no reservations attached because of gender, race, age, physical or mental handicap, religion, or ethnicity. It is a reflection of the common law's insistence on fundamental fairness. It hardens American *kaizen* into a true discipline of caring.

Through the elements of due care (guided learning experience), due diligence (prevention of problems), and due regard (respect and caring for each person) American *kaizen* becomes a system of caring in which

(*1*) Each person knows what is expected of him or her and has an opportunity to influence, but not decide, what is expected. The step is symbolized as KOE (Knowledge of Expectations).

(*2*) Each person must be given proactive assistance to successfully meet each expectation. The proviso, "what works," is KOA (Knowledge of Assistance).

(*3*) Each person is given timely feedback to know how well the expectations are being met. Timely knowledge of results is the basic principle for mastery of any skill, attitude, or knowledge. This element is KOR (Knowledge of Results) without which no one can be an effective learner.

(*4*) Each person must be guided to successful learning through the joint development of a corrective action plan matched to expectations not being satisfactorily met. This element is KOCA (Knowledge of Corrective Action).

(*5*) Each person must be given multiple chances to succeed. A reasonable person — the hallmark of common law — knows that it takes time to master new skills, attitudes, and knowledge. KOMC (Knowledge of Many Chances).

American *kaizen* is a system of three basic, common law elements—due care, due diligence, and due regard—whose purpose is the continuous improvement of human capital through successful learning. For all those who wish to, or are required to, produce or help people to learn what they need to know and be able to do, American *kaizen* provides an authoritative demonstrated successful approach.

THE GUIDED LEARNING EXPERIENCE: A WORKER TRAINING CRISIS IN WORLD WAR II

The power of the *guided learning experience* aspects of American *kaizen* can be observed through revisiting the *Training within Industry* program of World War II. A major phase of this program, called *Instructing the Workforce*—was a four-step sequence entitled *How to Instruct.* It was a universal process because it fit all training needs, regardless of product or service being needed for the war effort.

How to Instruct: A Universal Process of Training within Industry

(1) Step 1: Prepare the worker (Knowledge of Expectations).
- Put him or her at ease.
- State the job and find out what he or she already knows about it.
- Get him or her interested in learning the job.
- Place him or her in the correct position.

(2) Step 2: Present the operation (Knowledge of Assistance).
- Tell, show, and illustrate one important step at a time.
- Stress each key point.
- Instruct clearly, completely, patiently; but no more than he or she can master.

(3) Step 3: Try out performance (Knowledge of Results).
- Have him or her do the job. Correct errors.
- Have him or her explain the key point to you as he or she does the job again.
- Make sure he or she understands.
- Continue until you know he or she knows.

(4) Step 4: Follow up (Knowledge of Corrective Actions and Many Chances).
- Put him or her on his or her own. Designate a person to whom he or she goes for help.
- Check frequently. Encourage questions.
- Taper off extra coaching and close follow up.

The significant fact is that despite the vast variety of products, processes, operations, people, and the time pressures associated with the conduct of World War II (there were millions needed from all backgrounds and learning levels), these simple though profound rules fitted *all* work situations. They were truly "universals" on how to instruct for the on-the-job training experience. They were the steps in a universal process that led to the expertise (the human capital) needed to create what was called during the war an "Arsenal of Democracy."

WHY CALL THE PROCESS AN AMERICAN *KAIZEN?*

Kaizen is a Japanese word translated into English as meaning continuous improvement. The concept is believed by most management scholars and economists to be the key to Japan's post-war competitive success. Improvement is something that Americans generally take for granted or see as the product of some dramatic innovation, without necessarily paying attention to the speed of the change. Considering a continuum of improvement from abrupt to gradual, *kaizen* represents the gradual, even relentless or steady, pace.

> Nobody can stay the course without conscientious guidance from a skilled teacher and without the help of a Master. . . . All resistance I had to overcome, all inhibitions I had to fight down, before I succeeded.—Eugene Herrigel telling of his 6-year instruction in *Zen in the Art of Archery* (1953, p. 10)

Gradual change, so prevalent in the East, is not an obvious part of our Western way of life, in either the business or the public sectors. We seem to favor the abrupt, the breakthrough, the startling, the innovative, the bid for new ways. The key difference, therefore, in Japanese and American perspectives on how change is understood lies in this essence of the *kaizen* concept.

The Japanese cultural idea of *kaizen* is simple and straightforward. *Kaizen* means improvement, ongoing improvement involving everyone including managers and workers, leaders and followers. The *kaizen* philosophy assumes that a way of life, be it the working life, social life, or home life, deserves to be constantly improved. This very simple cultural "truth" is widely acknowledged to be a uniquely Japanese management practice.

But must it remain unique to the Japanese? Is there in fact an American counterpart, an American *kaizen* that might become widespread?

The basic argument presented here is that in our American culture there is a similar press for continuous improvement. It is focused through legal precedent on processes to protect certain fundamental rights that people are guaranteed under the Constitution.

The argument continues with a demonstration of how it is already applied to a protected class of public employees—school teachers. It then concludes with a discussion and demonstration that, were this concept revisited and more fully understood and applied widely in the American private and public sectors, it would represent a major way for mastering the new enriched knowledge and information economy brought on by the marriage of the computer to telecommunications.

CURRENT APPLICATION OF AMERICAN *KAIZEN*—A CASE STUDY

Public school teachers are a protected class by statute, interpretation of the 14th Amendment to the U.S. Constitution and the common law as codified in tort law. They have been ruled to have a property right in their positions and therefore may not be removed from their employment without due process (procedural and substantive). To terminate a public school teacher's employment, the employer must employ an American model of *kaizen*. Since the full framework is either unknown, neglected, or misunderstood, by those in responsible policy and executive roles, few teachers are ever removed, even for cause. Worse, as will be shown in what follows later, the failure to know and to use the American *kaizen* paradigm needlessly causes failure on the part of the students being served.

States are required by statute to make it very difficult for any public school teacher to fail, that is to lose his or her job. Before a teacher may be discharged, statute-driven steps must be documented by the administration and hearings held by the boards of education. The documentation that must be provided has to be of such a nature that a hearing officer or court will have detailed knowledge of the efforts of the administration in carrying out the American *kaizen* framework. The following section shows how the process is enforced by the courts in the case of a teacher being considered for employment termination.

(*1*) Step 1: Knowledge of Expectations (KOE): Each teacher must know what he or she is expected to do to be successful and how and when each expectation will be judged. Further, there must be documentation that the teacher has had an opportunity to influence, but not decide, what is required.

(*2*) Step 2: Knowledge of Assistance (KOA): Each teacher must have been given assistance in successfully meeting the expectations (KOE).

(*3*) Step 3: Knowledge of Results (KOR): Each teacher must be given timely feedback on how well or how poorly he or she is meeting what is expected (KOE), and if an expectation(s) has not been met satisfactorily, the principle of corrective action must be employed.

(*4*) Step 4: Knowledge of Corrective Action (KOCA): For each expectation *not* met satisfactorily as expressed in (KOR), a plan for specific corrective action must be developed with the teacher, and the sequence of the first three principles of American *kaizen* employed.

(*5*) Step 5: Knowledge of Many Chances (KOMC): The teacher must be given many chances to succeed before the final formal notice (the mandate procedural due process) is served. (Essentially a repetition of all the above.)

AMERICAN *KAIZEN* AND THE DISCIPLINE OF CARING—WHY CARE?

American *kaizen* is a true example of a discipline of caring. Discipline is used here to describe a body of knowledge. Caring is the fundamental emotion that supports life itself. Such an assertion then requires elaboration. But first, what is caring? In what sense can it be said to be discipline?

Caring centers on the relationship between people and between a person and what is perceived to be important—Coach Lombardi and his star rookie Larry Brown, for instance. It is the fundamental tie that binds someone who cares to an "other," whether that other be a person, a thing, a place, an enterprise, an idea, or an NFL running back.

The universal process of caring in its ideal form can be most adequately seen in that most basic of all life-supporting and life-enhancing relationships: the care of parents for their children. The process reveals that caring has a subject matter, a set of principles, practices, and even tools. It is a discipline in the same sense that a subject like physics or economics is a discipline.

There is an honest answer to the cynical question, "Why care?" There is an apt reply to the person who cites the cliché about something vital, "I couldn't care less." Through caring for others, for a community or the nation, for a place, for ideas, even for some things, we live the meaning of our lives. Without "cares," our lives are literally empty of meaning. Through caring and being cared for, we find our place in the world. Caring orders our values and our activities around it.

Caring can move us well above the level of narcissism and self-indulgence where both advertising and a permissive and indulgent society tends to anchor us. With an increase in caring, our egos shift from our center and enlarge to incorporate an "other." This enlargement strengthens the ego and lets us enter the state most aptly described by poets and artists. Infants and children evidently live on its level for a long time. In this level, the essence of each one of us can pass through the walls of the ego and slip out into animals or into trees, or an entire landscape. The poet William Wordsworth again and again felt something go out of him into the hills and come back to him. "I will look up to the hills," he wrote, "something from there comes to help me." Thoreau one day when it was raining wrote, "As the rain increases, this raindrop and I draw near to each other."

> In the sense in which a person can ever be said to belong in the world, he is at home not through dominating, or explaining or even appreciating, but through caring and being cared for. — Milton Meyerhoff, *On Caring* (1972, pp. 2–3)

Declaring American *kaizen* as a discipline of caring centers on its three interrelated elements—due care, due diligence, and due regard—to achieve successful learning. In combination, these elements form a system for assuring that people have the competence, confidence, and caring needed to succeed in a world that is growing in complexity and therefore, by definition, growing in the need for continuous improvement of learning.

Most discussions on attempts at improving human performance give short shrift to the true concept of "caring." Dictionary definitions identify it as the action of the verb "care," and "care" has a number of definitions ranging from a burdensome sense of responsibility, to painstaking attention, to loving or liking, and to perfunctory management or custody "as under a physician's care." Yet, caring implies more than perfunctory concern. It implies a broader concern for the whole person rather than just for a person's particular problem.

The skilled improvement of learning in homes, schools, and workplaces – the mission of American *kaizen* – is clearly a demonstration of skilled caring. Such caring is founded on the mastery of its discipline. The conclusion that American *kaizen* embodies caring can be safely made.

AMERICAN *KAIZEN* IN MEDICINE

Some of the history of medicine and the processes used by helping physicians to care for patients illuminates the power of American *kaizen* as a ubiquitous setting for the continuing improvement of human performance. A family example of one of the authors provides insights into important aspects of that medical history.

Samuel Lessinger was born in 1886. In 1910, at the age of 24, he became a pharmacist. Four years later, he began his practice as a physician.

He told vivid stories of his training and medical practice. He showed how he rolled his own pills, the nature of the pharmacopoeia, and the prevalent medical practice of expecting doctors to stay with a woman during the last stages of her pregnancy.

The year he died, 1966, he estimated that he would probably know less than 10% of the preparations physicians were then using. He was willing to concede that the young doctors knew more than he did at their age, but he wondered if they still had *compassio medici,* a basic regard for the human condition.

What Samuel Lessinger wondered about were the qualities he had in abundance and which the great physicians of the pre-scientific/technological era required in a doctor.

Dr. Francis Peabody (1927) observed in his classical dissertation:

> The most common criticism made at present by older practitioners is that young graduates have been taught a great deal about the mechanism of disease, but little about the practice of medicine – or, to put it more bluntly, they are too "scientific" and do not know how to take care of patients.

The good physician knows his patients through and through, and his knowledge is bought dearly. Time, sympathy and understanding must be lavishly dispensed, but the reward is to be found in the personal bond which forms the greatest satisfaction of the practice of medicine. One of the essential qualities of the clinician is interest in humanity, *for the secret of the care of the patient is in caring for the patient.* (pp. 877–882, emphasis added)

In this country, 1910 can safely be used as the benchmark to mark the transformation of medical practice from what it had been from the dawn of recorded time to what it has now become. The year Lessinger opened his drug store, 1910, the famous *Flexner Report* was published. By the time he began his medical practice, the Flexner "revolution" in medical training was spreading across the land. The revolution placed the major stress in training on knowledge and use of scientific principles to enable the achievement of technical proficiency. When doctors became medical scientists and technicians, they added two others to the potential of their primary "C" of caring: competence and confidence.

How fares the first one, caring, near the end of the century that began the revolution in medicine? And what does caring in medicine really mean?

There are numerous examples of physicians who are absolutely superb technicians, with all the latest knowledge and skill, but who approach patients in such a cold manner as to prompt doubt and distress. Members of medical society boards of censors are keenly aware that patients are often so unhappy with that kind of care that they file a formal grievance. In the investigation of such complaints, it becomes clear that, more often than not, the breakdown has been in the "caring" aspect of the physician-patient relationship—not in the quality of technical care and treatment provided.—Walter Menninger, The Menninger Foundation, Institute of Medicine of the National Academy of Sciences, Washington, D.C., 1974

Medical scholars have shown that the skills involved in caring for a patient can be acquired. This is why it is a sound assertion to think of caring as a discipline. For the physician, caring begins with the dictum *primum non nocere:* above all, do not harm.

Medical research, too, indicates that there is a universal method for successfully training interns and physicians of all kinds in skilled caring for patients. It has five steps remarkably similar to those in American *kaizen* applied to education:

(*1*) Establish clearly defined objectives in performance terms that both the trainers and the learners can recognize when they have achieved success.

(*2*) Teach the parts and the whole in an organized, progressive way.

(*3*) Integrate the particular aspect of training with the overall training.

(*4*) Provide ongoing clinical experience for the student to allow practice for mastery.

(*5*) Provide ongoing standardized evaluation of student progress with feedback to the student and opportunity to develop skills through additional practice.

As observations about the caring of physicians clearly show, there is a broader issue here. An identical case for the three "Cs" — competence, confidence, and caring — i.e., for a discipline of caring can be made for teaching and managing. The human organism is simply not designed to survive very well in any environment that treats it like an object.

Cairnes (1949), in describing a good doctor wrote:

> "He is a person who never spares himself in the interest of his patients; and in addition he is a man who studies the patient not only as a case but also as an individual." (p. 665)

Similarly, an apt description of a good teacher.

RELATIONSHIPS: THE STUFF OF LIFE

Relationships are the primary stuff of life. The degree of success of a life is in large measure a function of the quality of those relationships.

Caring transforms all relationships whether they be with people, with living things, with objects, with places, with organizations, or with ideas. It transforms through creating leaders who seek to serve the economic, the psychological, the physical, and the spiritual advantage of the one cared for.

Caring reflects love. It requires knowledge, dedication, faith, and patience. You know when you care. You know because there is a congruence between what you ought to do and what you want to do. You know because you are ready to respond to the needs of your "other." You know because you feel remorse if your "other" says, "Where were you when I needed you."

For the tough-minded, caring has additional value. The discipline of caring can directly affect the balance sheet. It definitely helps win football games. Such caring in any organization can decrease human failure, thus, saving costs and preventing harm.

The amount saved is roughly the average expenditure spent in dealing with each person who is not working at optimal level. The most critical, the amount of harm prevented, cannot be measured in dollars, but it can be surmised. It consists of the friction, the loss of morale, and the injury to the reputation of a team or organization that occurs from the actions of fearful, apathetic, sullen, or resentful people, who can be changed.

CHAPTER 4

Strategies for Honing America's Competitive Edge

FROM THE MID-1960s to the present, Americans have experienced a head-spinning period of technological, economic, and social change. There is dramatic evidence that change in the next 25 years should accelerate and be even more stressful.

These changes have come about from a massive transformation of the global economy. Third-world countries are rapidly going through the process of industrialization. They are entering Era 2, the Industrial Age, from which we are exiting. The advanced economies of Western Europe, North America, and Japan are rapidly evolving into Era 3 post-industrial knowledge economies. In this emerging new era, data and learning replace money and machines as the major *competitive advantage* of business. Creative intelligence underlies the wealth of this new era.

HUMAN CAPITAL: HISTORY AND EXPLORATION

Human capital is the basic energy of the new post-industrial global economy. American *kaizen* is the universal framework for continuous improvement of human capital. Human capital is the economist's term to describe skilled, educated people.

The concept of human capital was known to Adam Smith and other economists as early as the 18th century. Serious work on the economic theory of human capital, however, is relatively new. The term itself first appeared in scholarly literature in 1961 in an article in the *American Economic Review* entitled "Investment in Human Capital" by Nobel Prize-winning economist Theodore W. Schultz.

To some, it may seem foreign that knowledge can be considered a form of capital. The dictionary defines *capital* as "any form of wealth employed for the production of more wealth." Because of our immersion in the mindsets of the Industrial Age, it is common to think of a machine, like an auto assembly line, as capital equipment if it produces wealth. But physicians' skill and education also produce wealth for them in the form of considerably higher than average income, so medical knowledge and skill can be legitimately considered to be capital as well. Acquiring a medical education, then, is a major kind of capital investment. A doctor can be viewed as "capital knowledge" in human form or *human capital*. A similar statement can be made about anyone who has learned what he or she needs to know or be able to do to satisfy "customers."

This new economy we speak of requires an additional form of capital — intellectual capital. Schooling, if it is effective, a computer training course, expenditures in medical care, and training in the executive skills of thinking (e.g., problem solving, decision making) are capital as well. They improve health, thereby improving "mind" (mind/body is a unity), raising earnings, increasing quality of life, and leading to intrinsic motivation for work — a key requirement for quality both in product and service enterprises. Quality is, of course, one of the pillars of the new economy.

Four characteristics of knowledge and information make those men and women who are the embodiment of human capital adept at understanding and using the cognitive resources — the basic requirement for the emerging global economy:

(*1*) Knowledge is *expandable* and *self-generating*. The raw goods of an industrial economy are finite resources, such as fossil fuels.

(*2*) Knowledge is *substitutable*. It can and does replace land, labor, and physical and financial capital. A farmer who can grow more food on a specific piece of land using new farming techniques needs less land to increase production.

(*3*) Knowledge is *transportable*. A digital (electronic communications) economy moves knowledge to any location (on or near the earth) at the speed of light.

(*4*) Knowledge is *shareable*. Transfer of knowledge to others does not diminish its use by the sharer.

Our bureaucratically organized enterprises, both public and business, separate those who do the thinking, e.g., planning, rule making, problem solving, and decision making, from those who carry out the "orders."

All this is now undergoing change. In the new American economy, virtually every enterprise depends on various forms of data and information organized as knowledge. One can think immediately of patents, processes, management and leadership skills, technologies, information about customers and suppliers, information about government regulation and policy, economic forecasts, and market trends. The list is seemingly endless. Singly and together, these examples are forms of intellectual capital.

A useful metaphor to clarify the relationship between brainpower and intellectual capital is the analogy of a car and its driver. The car is the resource through which the driver can exercise his or her skill. Given two identical cars, the driver with the most skill will get the best results (safer driving, etc). The skill with which intellectual capital is used is the variable controlling brainpower. Unlike the car analogy, however, skilled thinking (the use of intellectual capital) serves *both* the utilization of and the generation of additional intellectual capital. It is for this reason that skilled thinking forms the cornerstone of any "think and work smarter" program.

It is fully consistent with the classical concept of capital in economics to say that investments in education, training, medical care, and other forms of stimulating *fitness for use* by human beings are investments in capital. To be sure, such capital formation produces a form of capital profoundly different from the commonly understood form. Unlike the physical and financial forms of capital, you cannot separate a person from his or her knowledge, skills, health, or values. Further, the intellectual component is precisely what is needed to work in an environment of accelerating change mediated by mind tools and information technology.

Thinking smarter has always been visible as a key asset in development of science and technology, whether smelting bronze thousands of years ago or writing software today. It can also be seen through a study of military and political heroes. It may be surprising to see what has been happening in the new economy.

Talk to CEOs today, and you will quickly discover that they will guard their research even more closely than they will their financial assets. You can see this as well in the services we buy.

Your lawyer doesn't charge his or her fees because the physical assets required of lawyering are so costly. Many businesses sell little else but thinking smarter: database publishers, software houses, consultants, advertising agencies, and investment counselors come to mind.

Today, the "thinking smarter" element in order to "work smarter" has entered into so-called mundane activities like preventive maintenance of household equipment and civic responsibility. The new economy demands flexibility, rapid adjustments to complexity and ambiguity, problem identification, team learning, and shared decision making—all "think and work smarter" requirements.

Clearly, an essential of this new economy is intellectual capital—the knowledge and skills of the work force. The foundation and development of that capital is cognitive ability, both knowledge and skilled thinking in its use.

At its core, intellectual capital is simply people who can think smarter in the way they gather and use information, make choices, and take responsibility. It can be seen also in their ability to work harmoniously and collaboratively with others.

AMERICAN *KAIZEN:* LINKING BREAKTHROUGH AND CONTROL

Earlier, we touched on how American *kaizen* can become the leading economic weapon in the fiercely competitive global economy. It is, after all, a basic and universal process for developing the essential energy of the new economy—human capital, men and women who are able to think and work smarter. There is another relationship of American *kaizen* to the productive management of organizations: the phenomena of breakthrough and control.

As Juran brilliantly established, all American managerial activity, prior to the onslaught of effective Japanese competition, was rightly thought to be directed at either breakthrough or control. "Managers are busy doing both of these things, and nothing else," wrote Juran.

- *Breakthrough* is innovation, change to something new and presumably something developing higher levels of achievement.

- *Control* is the prevention of change. It means achieving quotas, specifications, budgets, and schedules.

Breakthrough and control are part of one continuing cycle of events. The events consist of alternating plateaus of stability followed by gains in performance. The gains are the result of innovations; the plateaus are the result of control. The important insight we have gained from Japanese competition is that an either-or, win-lose, or zero-sum stance, typical of American management, while useful at times, is not sufficient. In the new economy, there is need to link continuous improvement to the managerial processes of breakthrough and control. In the new economy, this can be done only by attending to the nurturing of human capital on a continuing basis. American *kaizen* makes this possible.

In football, breakthrough is a first down or a score; control is avoiding a turnover (pass interception or fumble) and keeping your opponent from gaining ground or scoring.

Now, as one might say to a friend or colleague on a cold winter's evening, let's move our chairs a little closer to the fire and carefully examine these twin elements—breakthrough and control as united by American *kaizen*.

FIRST, THE CONTROL ELEMENT

Juran has shown that control means staying on course, adhering to standards, preventing change. Under complete control, literally nothing would change; we would be in a static condition, which is possible only in a quiescent world. This isn't as bad as it may sound to many Americans sold on innovation and change. In reality, there are many things that would be wonderful if we had no change.

Look at some of the things that are now so bothersome in our economy: downsizing, failing to meet targets, losing market share. Of course the word "static" has a bad connotation because it includes an implication of "no progress." There are some better words—aliases. We can use terms that sound more appealing: orderly, settled, predictable.

"Prevention of change" implies the existence of an accepted standard. The equivalent words for standard are quota, specification, budget, and schedule. In fact, the changes we are trying to prevent are departures in the wrong direction from these kinds of standards.

Control also offers us an unkind deception. Control may become a built-in procedure for avoiding progress, because we can become so preoccupied with meeting the existing standards that we fail to challenge the targets themselves. Meeting monthly and quarterly sales budgets to the disregard of all else has become the "siren song" of American business as it fights to keep from breaking up through the rude shocks of change.

NEXT, BREAKTHROUGH

Again, according to Juran, breakthrough is defined as change—a dynamic and decisive movement to new, higher levels of performance or accomplishment. The fact that breakthrough yields improvement does not necessarily mean that all improvement results solely from it. Improvement can certainly result from better control. It certainly can be the result of the process of American *kaizen* itself. An example of linking breakthrough and control follows.

- Suppose we have a procedure for notifying parents when their child is having difficulty in school. We make a strenuous effort to adhere to the procedure for fully notifying parents in a timely fashion. The blunders, short-cuts, missed deadlines, etc., are reduced systematically by processes of American *kaizen.*
- Someone comes up with a new approach to preventing student failure based on a different strategy or concept or set of practices from what works. Through the impact of American *kaizen* we find the means to cut failure significantly from the baseline of typical expectation.

The variety of improvements in both breakthrough and control triggered by American *kaizen* is as broad as the imagination and knowledge.

RESTORING A FORM OF AMERICAN "COMMON SENSE"

By revisiting the common law, we gain greater insight into its basis in common sense. The common law is America's storehouse of practical, and legal, wisdom. That storehouse, which we inherited from England and enriched through more than 200 years of the American experience, provides the principles that govern our relationships as citizens. Common law has given us such common sense-to-us-ideas that reasonable people can judge what is right and what is wrong behavior or that people should be judged fairly and held to be innocent until proven guilty.

> The common law is not a set of statutes developed by legislators. It is the synthesis of standards for human behavior derived from countless court decisions made over centuries.

- We must drive our cars reasonably or else be accountable for those we injure.
- We are entitled to be judged by a jury of our peers.
- Decisions about us are derived from asking what a *reasonable* person would do in such circumstances.
- The accident caused by swerving to avoid an oncoming vehicle, for example, is excusable; falling asleep or being intoxicated and causing an accident is not.

These merely illustrate the practical wisdom integrated into the common law that most Americans would say represents "common sense."

To enlarge on one of the examples, it was out of the common law that the jury system was developed—a group of peers who would together be expected to make a *reasonable* judgment as to a defendant's guilt or innocence. The most important standard in the common law is what a *reasonable person* would do in this particular situation. More than anything else, this idea of a reasonable person is held in the highest regard. The backbone of tort law, the codification of the common law with respect to negligence, for example, uses the notion of reasonableness to assess the degree of negligence in particular cases.

The common law is the opposite of ironclad rules that supposedly guarantee certain results. Instead, the guideposts it lays down are thought to be influenced always by the circumstances under investigation. This makes the common law inherently flexible and progressive. By nature, it evolves with new court decisions and with changing times.

> Supreme Court Justice Benjamin Cardozo, considered the greatest common law judge of the 20th century, said that the common law "is at bottom the philosophy of pragmatism."

WHAT COULD BE MORE AMERICAN
THAN PRAGMATISM?

Pragmatism is a philosophy grounded in the American tradition and was, in fact, developed by two distinguished Americans, Charles S. Pierce and William James. It is a movement whose basic doctrine is "that the meaning of an idea or a proposition lies in its observable practical consequences." What could be more American than this practical, matter-of-fact way of approaching or assessing situations or of solving problems?

Americans have, in large measure, enjoyed the promise of this great country: life, liberty, and the pursuit of happiness. The Constitution guarantees freedom, and the common law guarantees justice. And, as emphasized repeatedly, three seminal principles of the common law—*due care, due diligence, due regard*—form the core attributes of American *kaizen*. Skillful employment of this cultural ideal with management processes can give Americans the same results that the concept of *kaizen* brought to post-World War II Japan.

A WARNING

Thanks to awesome new information technologies, we become overwhelmed by data. Data are neither information nor knowledge. They are certainly not wisdom. It takes high levels of human capital to extract the potential for information, knowledge, and wisdom that is embedded in data. The following brief explanation makes this important and present technological danger clear.

- *Data* are symbols that represent the properties of objects or events. Cash receipts, inventory counts, and cases of disease are data.
- *Information* consists of mentally processed data, often in the form of tables and graphs. Groups of data increase their

usefulness in conveying information. Information is contained in descriptions that help give answers to questions of who, what, when, where, and how many. (Gasoline consumption data captured in the summer and in the winter serve as information for supply and demand forecasts for economists and oil refiners.) Like data, information represents the properties of objects and events.

- *Knowledge* is specific information about something. The term knowledge means the use of symbolic processes. These symbols may refer to words, special codes, pictures, or any other symbolic representation of a cue, concept, or principle. Knowledge is conveyed by *instructions* that direct people to answers about "how-to" questions. *Understanding* is conveyed by *explanations*. One has understanding when there are answers to "why" questions.

- *Wisdom* depends on judgment. It is distinguished from understanding, knowledge, information, and data by its introduction of the concept of *value*. Knowledge without understanding is potentially dangerous. Understanding without wisdom is greatly limited.

AN ORDINARY EXAMPLE IN ACTION

Most drivers now learn to drive a car with an automatic transmission. If they have to drive a car with a stick shift, they find themselves at a loss. They can turn to an instruction manual to get the knowledge. They can secure advice from someone who knows how. Armed with that knowledge, they might get the car in motion, perhaps with some lurching if they haven't got the hang of the clutch. Clearly, this shows a lack of skill. To operate a standard transmission effectively, the driver must know and get the feel of what happens when the clutch pedal is depressed. Until one has grasped these mechanical relationships, difficulties can be expected. All this is what is meant by understanding.

With understanding, confidence can grow even when the most difficult task faced by the stick shift driver happens: parallel parking facing up a hill! It is a challenge because we have to use judgment in sizing up the situation and then apply what we know and understand. It takes skill and experience to do it right. That is wisdom.

The actual driving of a car demonstrates that knowledge and skill are necessary, but not sufficient. Think of problems encountered due to traffic, weather conditions, road hazards, and so forth.

In the continuous improvement of human capital, the direction of the efforts must always move from data to information to knowledge and understanding. The crowning achievement, of course, is the fostering of wisdom.

Data → Information → Knowledge → Understanding → Wisdom

CONTINUOUS IMPROVEMENT IN HOMES, SCHOOLS AND WORKPLACES

It is our contention that if the continuous improvement of human capital process, now mandated as protections for teachers, were clearly seen, adopted, and internalized as our cultural approach to the continuous improvement of all human performance, not only would protections for teachers be strengthened but better learning for all "customers of education"—the students, their parents, and employers—would also result. The following amplifies this premise as it applies to classrooms. A similar case can be shown for learning achievement in homes and workplaces.

GUIDED LEARNING EXPERIENCE: DUE CARE IN ACTION

Through the application of American *kaizen*, each teacher (instructor, director, parent, boss, physician, lawyer—the list of potential "helpers" is seemingly endless):

Makes it clear to everybody just what the end product skill or knowledge will be (KOE, Knowledge of Expectations).

- If teachers want students to be able to repair an automobile part or sail a steady course, they show them how and make sure that they have the "end product" well in mind.
- The same is true if they are teaching students how to solve equations, write grammatical sentences, or design experiments.

- Many teachers learned a long time ago if they tell and show the students exactly what it is they want them to be able to do, they often won't have to tell them anything else.
- Many a school or college course has changed direction when the objectives were hammered out carefully between teachers and students in clear terms.

> Teachers let everybody know how each objective is going to be tested.

- The more information teachers give students about how they are expected to be tested, the more easily and quickly they can develop the required skills.
- Teachers sometimes are disinclined to let the student know what the test is. Probably they find themselves worrying at the thought of giving away the test. They are probably in a *teach about* mode rather than a *teach how* mode.
- There are very few skills that are taught where a teacher can't let the student know what the skills are and how they are to be tested.
- It is only when they are teaching *about* (and are using the test as a sample of what the student can say about the subject) that they have to guard the nature of the test.
- With American *kaizen,* teachers eliminate the opponent relationship between student and instructor, and the quickest way to do that is to be as direct and open about the nature of the test as a teacher can be.

> Teachers take advantage of what students know and can do when they come in.

- This important readiness factor can be determined by encouraging students to respond to expectations – a mandate included in Knowledge of Expectations.
- This is one of the aspects of American *kaizen* that almost everybody will agree with, but it's one of the hardest to implement.
- Teachers can find out what students can already do, and then they can productively use that information once they have it.
- Once the instruction is divided into the expectations (the skills

and knowledge—objectives—and the means of testing each skill and knowledge element is made known), the students can look at both the objective and test to decide if they have the skill or not. Here is where assistance comes in.

> With the American *kaizen* process of Knowledge of Assistance (KOA), teachers give students as many choices or paths through the instruction as possible.

- For example, if students are going to build a table, they would proceed in a certain order, from cutting to assembling to finishing. But if they were to learn the skills of table building, they could learn sanding and finishing skills first, or last, or in the middle somewhere.
- The tendency to teach in the same order as they are performed is strong, and yet a lot of enthusiasm can be dampened when teachers force students to put off parts that seem interesting to learn less interesting things first.
- *One of the primary attributes of American kaizen is always the affective one of wanting students to like the subject matter* (the effect of the due regard "lens").

> Teachers provide a range of materials, approach, and media whenever possible (Knowledge of Assistance).

- An instructor performs a certain number of functions—informing, showing how, providing feedback, counseling, and so on.
- Some of these functions are easier than others, and some can be done by computer, book, tape recorder, TV, or movie.
- It's desirable to use living human beings to the highest purpose.
- There should be no reluctance in augmenting the effectiveness of the instructor.

> Teachers allow enough time for any qualified individual to finish.

- One of the most counterproductive aspects of conventional schools is the fact that they are most often time-based rather than competency-based.

- Too often the students are started, ready or not, and after a period of time the instruction ceases whether or not the students have mastered the skill.
- The folly of this practice is made clear when attempts are then made to move the students on to new skills that depend on mastery of the old (the chronic problem of cumulative ignorance and learned helplessness).
- Instructors don't make mistakes like that when they teach someone to fly an airplane. The students work on landings until they can do them; the students master navigation before instructors let them practice cross-country flying. It seems that, as soon as teachers begin teaching *about* rather than *how*, they tend to push and prod the slower student to keep up with a time schedule and then cut him or her off when the time is up.
- With the exercise of American *kaizen,* teachers give students assurance that they have the time they need to read, ponder, practice, work out difficulties, look at other explanations, talk to other students—whatever they need to learn to do the skill.
- The other side of the coin is just as important. Students need to know that they are in a system designed so that if their interest catches fire they won't have to sit around and wait for others to catch up.

> Teachers provide a sort of "map" to keep students informed about where they are in the curriculum.

- Teachers know this, yet not many take the simple step of providing and continuously updating a course "map."

> Teachers provide opportunity for practice of the skill being taught.

> There is strong temptation, when designing instruction, for teachers to tell students exactly how to perform a skill, what to watch out for, and how to tell when they are doing it right, but not to provide space and time for students actually to practice under their guidance.

> Teachers provide feedback to students on their practice.

- Teachers not only provide practice of a skill, but ensure that students know directly if they are practicing correctly or not and if not, why not (Knowledge of Results).

> Under American *kaizen,* teachers test and assess often and in a non-threatening way.

- When students dream of an ideal teacher, one of the things they most often want to change is the brittle, enemy relationship between them and the instructor, brought about by the way some teachers test and grade. They want a teacher who is fundamentally fair and gives them respect—the essence of due regard.
- Two things help: first, teachers should test often, so that students don't have to accumulate too much before they find out if they are on the right track. Second, teachers should test in a nonthreatening manner by informing students accurately what the test will be like, by letting students pick their own time for testing when feasible, by giving timely constructive feedback on the results of the test, and by letting students keep testing until the desired skill has been demonstrated.
- Under American *kaizen,* teachers accept feedback from the students and from colleagues for self-correction. They know that no one and no system is perfect.

> In the exercise of American *kaizen,* teachers compare each student to expected objectives. They are interested in individual mastery, not solely some group average.

- Optimum acceptability of any student's achievement should be what is necessary to flourish in the new Era 3 Age. Wherever it is set, the comparison of the student's skill should be to that standard.
- Teachers must not make the familiar conventional mistake of changing standards based on what some other student did on the test, as illustrated by grading on a bell-shaped curve of

probability or chance, thus assuring that an appropriate number are expected to do poorly or fail.

THE SEVERAL "FACES" OF AMERICAN *KAIZEN*

> American *kaizen* has several aliases that bear directly on the management and improvement of learning and leadership.

From the framework of management, the principles of expectations, assistance, results, corrective action, and many chances of due care expressed as guided learning experience form the best features of MBO – Management by Objectives.

For specialists in educational psychology and instructional design, due care fits the essential steps of the *basic practice strategy* also known as *direct instruction,* found through careful research to be the most effective way to improve the learning of skills.

American *kaizen* introduces into education the neglected concept of *quality control* – the foundation of *accountability for results.* It does this because the sum and substance of quality control is feedback of results followed by timely corrective action. The common thermostat found in many homes shows how this works.

The target range of a room thermostat is between 68 and 72 degrees. This range has been found empirically to be the most comfortable. The target sets the expectations for room temperature. There is a lever enabling a person to set the objective.

The device has a sensor that can signal for assistance when the target is not being met satisfactorily. When there is a gap between expectation and results, the sensor (*alias* test, exam, assessment) sends a signal to a source of assistance – a heat pump that can supply hot or cold air as needed. The thermostat is a temperature *system,* it is programmed for corrective action and has unlimited chances to be successful.

The story of the blind man and the elephant bears repeating. A blind man was asked to describe how an elephant looks. Upon grabbing the elephant's tail, he offered that the elephant must look like a rope. After wrapping his arms around one of its legs, he said the animal must look

like a large tree. Then, asked to hold the elephant's ear, he now concluded this animal must look like a leaf. To those only able to "see"
their part of the system, the system and the behavior of its parts remain
elusive.

THE ALIASES OF AMERICAN *KAIZEN* SHOW ITS INTERDISCIPLINARY NATURE

We know now that, in addition to its legal framework, American
kaizen is a discipline of caring. We also see that it reflects and illuminates principles from management, engineering, and instruction.
It is safe to say that it is, in significant ways, an artifact of American
culture.

Human Capital

The source of human capital formation and its optimal employment
is learning. Human capital is the economic term for men and women
trained and educated in the understanding and use of cognitive
qualities: reasoning, problem solving, thinking, and choice making.
High level cognition is a learned phenomenon. The pragmatic application of *human capital* is men and women who "think and work
smarter."

Kaizen

Kaizen is a Japanese cultural concept, the English translation of
which is *continuous improvement*. It is a shared cultural understanding
among the people of Japan that comes "naturally" to them through
direct teaching and reinforcement at home, at school, and in the workplace. Until this time, one of the prime elements in the Japanese global
competitive advantage in product, promotion, and sale is *kaizen*. We
see the impact of *kaizen* in action in the continuous improvement of
small details in Japanese products—cars, electronics, and cameras.

DIVERSITY MEANS STRENGTH

The United States, a nation of diverse populations, does not have such a shared cultural concept. It is neither taught nor reinforced as is done in Japan. Our nation, founded in the law, the Constitution, and the common law, has developed a potential equivalent to the concept of Japanese *kaizen*. We call it here, American *kaizen*.

Particular emphasis has been given to learning, because it is central to the new economy. Learning is a before and after happening. You cannot define a word, or fix something, or solve a problem *before* you have learned. You can define it, or fix it, or solve it, *after* you have learned. Such a description, while true, neglects the most critical factor in all learning: *the learning experience.*

Although learning occurs from cradle to grave, if we do not focus on the experience from which it flows, we fail to give the learning process much thought. While we might recognize *what* we have learned, if we give little or no thought to *how* we learn, we lose the key opportunity to continually learn more.

The class of learning experience called *trial and error* helps us relate to having learned some things that way. But the most efficient and effective learning experience is that provided by an informed and practiced person in an appropriate setting. That person is a guide with a variety of names — parent, teacher, coach, doctor, just to name a few.

The principal places in our society where learning guides function are in the home, school, and workplace. American *kaizen* can be practiced in each of these principal places by parents, teachers, and employers separately. Practiced in partnership and alliances through a shared understanding of the process, American *kaizen* would provide the quantum leap to the nation's competitive advantage required in the new economy.

CHAPTER 5

The Sports Metaphor in Action

TELEVISION HAS GIVEN thousands of viewers an unparalleled opportunity to watch action-packed sports. Whether it be a college or professional game, what may be hidden to the typical viewer is the immense variety of factors at work among a team of players on the field that makes them capable of winning consistently.

Seldom have a sport and a medium for its presentation meshed so neatly as professional football and television. Football is, to coin a word, *telegenic*. Viewers participate vicariously in the essential conflict that makes pro football so popular. There were great players and fabulous games before the TV marriage, but great as they were, comparatively few fans knew about them. TV makes today's superstars, as well as the essence of the game itself, familiar to the nation. And, it is the power of the sports metaphor that makes it the nation's communicator of key ideas.

Among others, it is the mastery of many subtleties that mold a serious player—to learn how to quickly and positively adapt to a constantly changing game.

Top-notch players couple knowledge of fundamentals with superior physical and mental conditioning. They always make "their practices"—their mandated sessions of repetition and drill. Every world-class athlete, irrespective of his or her chosen sport, grasps the need for *continuous learning*.

> "Game management is a lost art. Game management is an art form. Some coaches hit it beautifully, others very poorly, in the sense the game can get away from the head coach."—Coach Bill Walsh, San Francisco 49ers

Football is a science as well as an art. Each player knows that he can not defeat the team's opponent alone. Every successful play must have the precision of a finely tuned machine. A player knows that his every move, block, fake, run, catch, throw, or tackle is just part of that "machine." He also knows that all of these actions are for naught if his teammates fail in their own individual tasks.

Football is an example of an ultimate team sport. The *playbook* synthesizes the principles, strategies, practices, and tools of such sports. As the game unfolds, the coach calibrates the strategy and adjusts the tactics as one would the wall thermostat. Teamwork and timing are crucial to winning. The lack of these basic ingredients is often the reason for defeat. This brings to mind the NFL maxim: on any given day, any team can beat any other team.

CHANGE AND THE SPORTS PERSPECTIVE

Through professional sports, we can observe the impact of gradual and rapid change as it affects an entire *system.*

In sports, systems thinking is the foundation of breakthrough (innovation) and control (stability). Together they add up to continuous improvement. It can best be understood by contrasting it to the nonsystem approach used in education and Era 2 business ventures.

In education, innovation is a one-shot, event-oriented phenomenon in which the emphasis is on the challenge of getting some discrete change installed, accepted, and used. From this perspective, change is regarded as an unusual, novel, periodic event interposed between long periods of stability. It is episodic.

By comparison, in sports, innovation is a normal function of the enterprise. It is therefore provided for as an expected and routine occurrence. Further, it is perceived to be a *system-changing* process.

In sports, change to the system may result from (1) changed performance requirements either of players or of the rules or procedures of the game, (2) availability of improved technology, and (3) discovery of procedural errors in an operating system.

Whatever the reason for a proposed change, it is viewed as a process whose "ripple effect" on all parts of the system must be painstakingly examined. Personnel roles, hardware, and procedures must be evaluated in light of the proposed change and, if needed, redesigned to support what the change actually triggers—a new system.

And the benefits that follow from a new system may have far-reaching effects in other spheres. The search by coaches for the essential building blocks of the performance system and their critical sequencing, for example, inevitably directs the coaches to the acceptance of the importance of *first learnings*. This perspective has special significance for education, for *basic* learnings, and for *remedial* instruction. A good beginning multiplies its advantages for a lifetime.

In many instances, a successful coach defines and designs an entirely different approach for the team that has a losing season or in the case of a particular player, who is not up to par as a professional player. What the coach then produces is likely to be a breakthrough (something different that is marketable and is an addition to the professional storehouse of "what works for winning" — a *professional praxis* — the inventory of good practice for getting results).

SYSTEMS THINKING

Optimum implementation of an innovation requires systems thinking. One change can or should begin a chain reaction that shakes the structure of the entire system. The history of innovations in schools (and government of which they are a principal representative) is quite unlike that in an applied field like football in which there are functional products and quality control.

> Generally speaking we find that people perceive correctly their immediate environment. They know what they are trying to accomplish. They know the crises that will force certain actions. They are sensitive to the power structure of the organization, to the traditions, and to their own personal goals and welfare. In general, when circumstances are conducive to frank disclosure, people can state what they are doing and can give rational reasons for their actions. In many instances it emerges that the known policies describe a system that actually causes the troubles. In other words, the known and intended practices of the organization are fully sufficient to create the difficulty, regardless of what happens outside. . . . In fact, a downward spiral develops in which the presumed solution makes the difficulty worse and thereby causes redoubling of the presumed solution. — Jay W. Forrester, *Counterintuitive Behavior of Social Systems* (1975, p. 215)

It is no secret among educators that even the most critical curricular and instructional decisions are influenced mainly by other than educational considerations.

Professional leaders realize that all organizations are, at base, systems. They know that a decision made in one department usually affects other departments. Skillful executives learn not only how to recognize the impact of decisions on all parts of the organization but also what to do about it. Failure to think in this way can be expensive, even catastrophic, for the organization.

The systems approach is best described as a reasoned and total, rather than a fragmented, look at a problem or a challenge. All parts in any system are interrelated. An automobile is a system. A human being, a corporation, a state, a school, a team, all are systems. And especially the elephant.

> "Anything that consists of parts connected together will be called a system. For instance, a game of snooker is a system, whereas a single snooker ball is not. A car, a pair of scissors, an economy, a language, an ear, and a quadratic equation, all these things are systems. They can be pointed out as aggregates of bits and pieces, but they begin to be understood only when the connection between the bits and pieces, the dynamic interactions of the whole organism, are made the object of study."—Stafford Beer, English industrial consultant

If executives have only a vague idea of what a system is or what the systems approach does or what constitutes its counterintuitive nature of behavior, the effort at change will be hazardous. The concept is an important one in professional sports, especially in seeking solutions to complex problems and organizing to achieve large tasks.

Using the sports perspective, schools will be motivated to plan individualized curricula as a sequence of learned behaviors. This sharply contrasts with present and traditional practice, the curriculum for which is not a series of pupil behaviors. It is a series of *time exposures* to teaching.

What is required for schools under the sports perspective is clear:

- a shift in basic orientation from teaching offered to learning achieved
- fresh emphases and new tools for continuous improvement of learning through guided learning experience

- distinct strategies based on praxis—what works—to achieve student progress and the repair of instruction

THE PRAXIS OF EDUCATION: WHAT WORKS IN THE PLAYBOOK (33 PLAYS)

There is an inventory of *good practice* to achieve instruction. We know a great deal about what works in education. We can use this praxis, this set of authoritative practices verified by actual tryout, to ensure better results. They are the equivalent of successful plays in the football playbook metaphor.

The following thirty-three "plays" were drawn from the first-ever book of good practice published by the U.S. Department of Education under the title *What Works* (1986).

1—CURRICULUM OF THE HOME   WHAT WORKS

Research Finding: Parents are their children's first and most influential teachers. What parents do to help their children learn is more important to academic success than how well-off the family is.

Comment: Parents can do many things at home to help their children succeed in school. Unfortunately, recent evidence indicates that many parents are doing much less than they might. American mothers, on average, spend less than half an hour a day talking, explaining, or reading with their children. Fathers spend less than 15 minutes.

Parents can create a "curriculum of the home" that teaches their children what matters. They do this through daily conversations, household routines, attention to school matters, and affectionate concern for their children's progress.

Conversation is important. Children learn to read, reason, and understand things better when their parents

- read, talk, and listen to them
- tell them stories, play games, share hobbies
- discuss news, TV programs, and special events

In order to enrich the "curriculum of the home," some parents

- provide books, supplies, and a special place for studying
- observe routine for meals, bedtime, and homework
- monitor the amount of TV time and doing after-school jobs

Parents stay aware of their children's lives at school when they

- discuss school events
- help children meet deadlines
- talk with their children about school problems and successes

Research on both gifted and disadvantaged children shows that home efforts greatly improve student achievement. When parents of disadvantaged children take the above steps, their children can do as well at school as children of more affluent families.

2—READING TO CHILDREN   WHAT WORKS

Research Finding: The best way for parents to help their children become readers is to read to them, even when they are very young. Children benefit most from reading aloud when they discuss stories, learn to identify letters and words, and talk about the meanings of words.

Comment: The specific skills required for reading come from direct experience with written language. At home, as in school, the more reading the better.

Parents can encourage their children's reading in many ways. Some tutor informally by pointing out letters and words on signs and containers. Others use more formal tools, such as workbooks. But children whose parents simply read to them perform as well as those whose parents use workbooks or have had training in teaching.

The conversation that goes with reading aloud to children is as important as the reading itself. When parents ask children only superficial questions about stories or do not discuss the stories at all, their children do not achieve as well in reading as the children of parents who ask questions that require thinking and who relate the stories to everyday events. Kindergarten children who know a lot about written language usually have parents who believe that reading is important and who seize every opportunity to act on that conviction by reading to their children.

3—INDEPENDENT READING **WHAT WORKS**

Research Finding: Children improve their reading ability by reading a lot. Reading achievement is directly related to the amount of reading children do in school and outside.

Comment: Independent reading increases both vocabulary and reading fluency. Unlike using workbooks and performing computer drills, reading books gives children practice in the "whole act" of reading; that is, both in discovering the meanings of individual words and in grasping the meaning of an entire story. But American children do not spend much time reading independently at school or at home. In the average elementary school, for example, children spend just 7 to 8 minutes a day reading silently. At home, half of all fifth graders spend only 4 minutes a day reading. These same children spend an average of 130 minutes a day watching television.

Research shows that the amount of leisure time spent reading is directly related to children's reading comprehension, the size of their vocabularies, and the gains in their reading ability. Clearly, reading at home can be a powerful supplement to class work. Parents can encourage leisure reading by making books an important part of the home, by giving books or magazines as presents, and by encouraging visits to the local library.

Another key to promoting independent reading is making books easily available to children through classroom libraries. Children in classrooms that have libraries read more, have better attitudes about reading, and make greater gains in reading comprehension than children in classrooms without libraries.

4—COUNTING **WHAT WORKS**

Research Finding: A good way to teach children simple arithmetic is to build on their informal knowledge. This is why learning to count everyday objects is an effective basis for early arithmetic lessons.

Comment: Young children are comfortable with numbers; "math anxiety" comes in later years. Just watching the enjoyment children get from songs and nursery rhymes that involve counting is ample evidence of their natural ease. These early counting activities can set the stage for later, more formal, exposure to arithmetic.

Counting is not limited to merely reciting strings of numbers. It also includes matching numbers to objects and reaching totals (for example, counting the number of apples sitting on the table). Children learn to do arithmetic by first mastering different counting strategies, beginning with rote counting (1, 2, 3, 4) and progressing to memorized computations (2 x 2 = 4). As children learn the facts of arithmetic, they also learn to combine those facts by using more sophisticated strategies. As their skills grow, they rely less and less on counting.

When teachers begin by using children's informal knowledge, then proceed to more complex operations, children learn more readily and enjoy it.

5—EARLY WRITING   WHAT WORKS

Research Finding: Children who are encouraged to draw and scribble "stories" at an early age will later learn to compose more easily, more effectively, and with greater confidence than children who do not have this encouragement.

Comment: Even toddlers, who can hardly hold a crayon or pencil, are eager to "write" long before they acquire the skills in kindergarten that formally prepare them to read and write.

Studies of very young children show that their carefully formed scrawls have meaning to them and that this writing actually helps them develop language skills. Research suggests that the best way to help children at this stage of their development as writers is to respond to the ideas they are trying to express.

Very young children take the first steps toward writing by drawing and scribbling, or, if they cannot use a pencil, they may use plastic or metal letters on a felt or magnetic board. Some preschoolers may write on toy typewriters; others may dictate stories into a tape recorder or to an adult, who writes them down and reads them back. For this reason, it is best to focus on the intended meaning of what very young children write, rather than on the appearance of the writing.

Children become more effective writers when parents and teachers encourage them to choose the topics they write about, then leave them alone to exercise their own creativity. The industriousness of such children has prompted one researcher to comment that they "violate the child labor laws."

6—SPEAKING AND LISTENING   WHAT WORKS

Research Finding: A good foundation in speaking and listening helps children become better readers.

Comment: When children learn to read, they are making a transition from spoken to written language. Reading instruction builds on conversational skills: the better children are at using spoken language, the more successfully they will learn to read written language. To succeed at reading, children need a basic vocabulary, some knowledge of the world around them, and the ability to talk about what they know. These skills enable children to understand written material more readily.

Research shows a strong connection between reading and listening. A child who is listening well shows it by being able to retell stories and repeat instructions. Children who are good listeners in kindergarten and first grade are likely to become successful readers by the third grade. Good fifth-grade listeners are likely to do well on aptitude and achievement tests in high school.

Parents and teachers need to engage children in thoughtful discussions on all subjects—current events, nature, sports, hobbies, machines, family life, and emotions—in short, on anything that interests children. Such discussions should not be limited to reading selections that are part of class work.

Conversing with children about the world around them will help them reflect on past experiences and on what they will see, do, and read about in the future.

Speaking English at school is especially important for children who have not grown up speaking English.

7—DEVELOPING TALENT   WHAT WORKS

Research Finding: Many highly successful individuals have above-average, but not extraordinary, intelligence. Accomplishment in a particular activity is often more dependent upon hard work and self-discipline than on innate ability.

Comment: High academic achievers are not necessarily born smarter than others, nor do people born with extraordinary abilities necessarily become highly accomplished individuals. Parents, teachers, coaches, and the individuals themselves can influence how much a mind or talent develops by fostering self-discipline and encouraging hard work. Most highly successful individuals have above-average, but not exceptional, intelligence. A high IQ seems less important than specializing in one area of endeavor, persevering, and developing the social skills required to lead and get along well with others.

Studies of accomplished musicians, athletes, and historical figures show that when they were children, they were competent, had good social and communication skills, and showed versatility as well as perseverance in practicing their skill over long periods. Most got along well with their peers and parents. They constantly nurtured their skills. And their efforts paid off.

Developing talent takes effort and concentration. These, as much as nature, are the foundation for success.

8—IDEALS   WHAT WORKS

Research Finding: Belief in the value of hard work, the importance of personal responsibility, and the importance of education itself contributes to greater success in school.

Comment: The ideals that children hold have important implications for their school experiences. Children who believe in the value of hard work and repsonsibility and who attach importance to education are likely to have higher academic achievement and fewer disciplinary problems than those who do not have these ideals. They are also less likely to drop out of school. Such children are more likely to use their out-of-school time in ways that reinforce learning.

For example, high school students who believe in hard work, responsibility, and the value of education spend about 3 more hours a week on homework than do other students. This is a significant difference, since the average student spends only about 5 hours a week doing homework.

Parents can improve their children's chances for success by emphasizing the importance of education, hard work, and responsibility, and by encouraging their children's friendships with peers who have similar values. The ideals that students, their parents, and their peers hold are more important than a student's socioeconomic and ethnic background in predicting academic success.

9—GETTING PARENTS INVOLVED   WHAT WORKS

Research Finding: Parental involvement helps children learn more effectively. Teachers who are successful at involving parents in their children's schoolwork are successful because they work at it.

Comment: Most parents want to be involved with their children's schoolwork but are unsure of what to do, how to do it. Many say they would welcome more guidance and ideas from teachers. But it takes more than occasional parent-teacher conferences and school open houses to involve parents.

Teachers who are successful at promoting parent participation in the early grades use strategies like these:

- Some teachers ask parents to read aloud to the child, to listen to the child read, and to sign homework papers.
- Others encourage parents to drill students on math and spelling and to help with homework lessons.
- Teachers also encourage parents to discuss school activities with their children and suggest ways parents can help teach their children at home.

For example, a simple home activity might be alphabetizing books; a more complex one would be using kitchen supplies in an elementary science experiment.

Teachers meet parents' wishes for face-to-face contact by inviting them to the classroom to see how their children are being taught. This first-hand observation shows parents how the teacher teaches and gives parents ideas on what they can do at home.

10—PHONICS   WHAT WORKS

Research Finding: Children get a better start in reading if they are taught phonics. Learning phonics helps them to understand the relationship between letters and sounds and to "break the code" that links the words they hear with the words they see in print.

Comment: Until the 1930s and 1940s, most American children learned to read by the phonics method, which stresses relationships between spoken sounds and printed letters. Children learned the letters of the alphabet and the sounds those letters represent. For several decades thereafter, however, the "look-say" approach to reading was dominant: children were taught to identify whole words in the belief that they would make more progress if they identified whole words as adults seem to. Recent research indicates that, on the average, children who are taught phonics get off to a better start in learning to read than children who are not taught phonics.

Identifying words quickly and accurately is one of the cornerstones of skilled reading. Phonics improves the ability of children both to identify words and to sound out new ones. Sounding out the letters is the first tentative step of a toddler: it helps children gain a secure verbal footing and expand their vocabularies beyond limits of basic readers.

Because phonics is a reading tool, it is best taught in the context of reading instruction, not as a separate subject to be mastered. Good phonics strategies include teaching children the sounds of letters in isolation and in words (s/i/t), and how to blend the sounds together (s-s-i-i-t).

Phonics should be taught early but not overused. If phonics instruction extends for too many years, it can defeat the spirit and excitement of learning to read. Phonics helps children pronounce words approximately, a skill they can learn by the end of second grade. In the meantime, children can learn to put their new phonics skills to work by reading good stories and poems.

11—READING COMPREHENSION   WHAT WORKS

Research Finding: Children get more out of a reading assignment when the teacher precedes the lesson with background information and follows it with discussion.

Comment: Young readers, and poor readers of every age, do not consistently see connections between what they read and what they already know. When they are given background information about the principal ideas or characters in a story before they read it, they are less apt to become sidetracked or confused and are more likely to understand the story fully. Afterwards, a question and answer session clarifies, reinforces, and extends their understanding.

Good teachers begin the day's reading lesson by preparing children for the story to be read—introducing the new words and concepts they will encounter. Many teachers develop their own introductions or adapt those offered in teachers' manuals.

Such preparation is like a road map: children need it because they may meet new ideas in the story and because they need to be alerted to look for certain special details. Children who are well prepared remember a story's ideas better than those who are not.

In the discussion after the reading lesson, good teachers ask questions that probe the major elements of the story's plot, characters, theme, or moral. ("Why did Pinocchio's nose grow? Why did he lie? What did his father think about his lying? Did their feelings for each other change?") Such questions achieve two purposes: to check students' understanding of what they have just read and to highlight the meanings and ideas students should look for in future reading selections. These questions lay the path for later appreciation of literature theme and style. When children take part in a thought-provoking story discussion, they understand more clearly that the purpose of reading is to get information and insight, not just to decode the words on a page.

12—SCIENCE EXPERIMENTS   **WHAT WORKS**

Research Finding: Children learn science best when they are able to do experiments, so they can witness "science in action."

Comment: Reading about scientific principles or having a teacher explain them is frequently not enough. Cause and effect are not always obvious, and it may take an experiment to make that clear. Experiments help children actually see how the natural world works.

Scientific explanations sometimes conflict with the way students may suppose that things happen or work. For example, most students would probably think that a basketball will fall faster than a ping-pong ball because the basketball is larger and heavier. Unless a teacher corrects this intuitive assumption by having the students perform an experiment and see the results, the students will continue to trust their intuition, even though the textbook or the teacher tells them the effect of gravity on both objects is exactly the same and that both will reach the floor at the same instant.

Many students have misconceptions even after taking a science course, because they have not had opportunities to test and witness the evidence that would change their minds. To clear up misconceptions, students need to be given the chance to predict the results they anticipate in an experiment. For example, the mistaken idea that the basketball will fall faster than the ping-pong ball can be tested experimentally. The teacher can then explain why the original hypothesis was faulty. In this way, experiments help students use the scientific method to distinguish facts from opinions and misconceptions.

13—STORYTELLING   **WHAT WORKS**

Research Finding: Telling young children stories can motivate them to read. Storytelling also introduces them to cultural values and literary traditions before they can read, write, and talk about stories by themselves.

Comment: Elementary school teachers can introduce young students to the study of literature by telling them fairy tales such as the

Three Billy Goats Gruff or *Beauty and the Beast* and myths such as *The Iliad*. Even students with low motivation and weak academic skills are more likely to listen, read, and write, and work hard in the context of storytelling.

Stories from the real tradition celebrate heroes who struggle to overcome great obstacles that threaten to defeat them. Children are neither bored nor alienated by learning literature through storytelling; they enjoy, understand, and sympathize naturally with the goats on the bridge, Beauty in a lonely castle, and Hector and Achilles outside the walls of Troy. With the help of skillful questioning, they can also learn to reflect on the deeper meanings of these stories.

Children also benefit from reading stories aloud and from acting out dramatic narration, whether at home or at school. Parents can begin reading to their children as infants and continue for years to come.

Storytelling can ignite the imaginations of children, giving them a taste of where books can take them. The excitement of storytelling can make reading and learning fun and can instill in children a sense of wonder about life and learning.

14—TEACHING WRITING   **WHAT WORKS**

Research Finding: The most effective way to teach writing is to teach it as a process of brainstorming, composing, revising, and editing.

Comment: Students learn to write well through frequent practice. A well-structured assignment has a meaningful topic, a clear sense of purpose, and a real audience. Good writing assignments are often an extension of class reading, discussion, and activities, not isolated exercises.

An effective writing lesson contains these elements:

- *brainstorming:* Students think and talk about their topics. They collect information and ideas, frequently much more than they will finally use. They sort through their ideas to organize and clarify what they want to say.

- *composing:* Students compose a first draft. This part is typically time-consuming and hard, even for very good writers.
- *revising:* Students re-read what they have written, sometimes collecting responses from teachers, classmates, parents, and others. The most useful teacher response to an early draft focuses on what students are trying to say, not the mechanics of writing. Teachers can help most by asking for clarification, commenting on vivid expressions or fresh ideas, and suggesting ways to support the main thrust of the writing. Students can then consider the feedback and decide how to use it to improve the next draft.
- *editing:* Students then need to check their final version for spelling, grammar, punctuation, other writing mechanics, and legibility.

Prompt feedback from teachers on written assignments is important. Students are most likely to write competently when schools routinely require writing in all subject areas, not just in English class.

15—LEARNING MATHEMATICS   WHAT WORKS

Research Finding: Children in early grades learn mathematics more effectively when they use physical objects in their lessons.

Comment: Numerous studies of mathematics achievement at different grade and ability levels show that children benefit when real objects are used as aids in learning mathematics. Teachers call these objects "manipulatives."

Objects that students can look at and hold are particularly important in the early stages of learning a math concept because they help the student understand by visualizing. Students can tie later work to these concrete activities.

The type or design of the objects used is not particularly important; they can be blocks, marbles, poker chips, cardboard cutouts—almost anything. Students do as well with inexpensive or homemade materials as with costly, commercial versions.

The cognitive development of children and their ability to understand ordinarily move from the concrete to the abstract. Learning from real objects takes advantage of this fact and provides a firm foundation for the later development of skills and concepts.

16—ESTIMATING   **WHAT WORKS**

Research Finding: Although students need to learn how to find exact answers to arithmetic problems, good math students also learn the helpful skill of estimating answers. This skill can be taught.

Comment: Many people can tell almost immediately when a total seems right or wrong. They may not realize it, but they are using a math skill called estimating. Estimating can also be valuable to children learning math.

When students can make good estimates of the answer to an arithmetic problem, it shows they understand the problem. This skill leads them to reject unreasonable answers and to know whether they are "in the ballpark."

Research has identified three key steps used by good estimators. These can be taught to all students:

- Good estimators begin by altering numbers to more manageable forms—by rounding, for example.
- They change parts of a problem into forms they can handle more easily. In a problem with several steps, they may rearrange the steps to make estimation easier.
- They also adjust two numbers at a time when making their estimates. Rounding one number higher and one number lower is an example of this technique.

Before students can become good at estimating, they need to have quick, accurate recall of basic facts. They also need a good grasp of the place value system (ones, tens, hundreds, etc.).

Estimating is a practical skill; for example, it comes in very handy when shopping. It can also help students in many areas of mathematics and science that they will study in the future.

17—TEACHER EXPECTATIONS   WHAT WORKS

Research Finding: Teachers who set and communicate high expectations to all their students obtain greater academic performance from those students than teachers who set low expectations.

Comment: The expectations teachers have about what students can and cannot learn may become self-fulfilling prophecies. Students tend to learn as little—or as much—as their teachers expect.

Students from whom teachers expect less are treated differently. Such students typically

- are seated farther away from the teacher
- receive less direct instruction
- have fewer opportunities to learn new material
- are asked to do less work

Teachers also call on these students less often, and the questions they ask are more likely to be simple and basic rather than thought-provoking. Typically, such students are given less time to respond and less help when their answers are wrong. But when teachers give these same students the chance to answer more challenging questions, the students contribute more ideas and opinions to class discussions.

18—STUDENT ABILITY AND EFFORT   WHAT WORKS

Research Finding: Children's understanding of the relationship between being smart and hard work changes as they grow.

Comment: When children start school, they think that ability and effort are the same thing; in other words, they believe that if they work hard they will become smart. Thus, younger children who fail believe this is because they didn't try hard enough, not because they have less ability.

Because teachers tend to reward effort in earlier grades, children frequently concentrate on working hard rather than on the quality of their work. As a result, they may not learn how to judge how well they are performing.

In later elementary grades, students slowly learn that ability and effort are not the same. They come to believe that lower ability requires harder work to keep up and that students with higher ability need not work so hard. At this stage, speed at completing tasks replaces effort as the sign of ability; high levels of effort may even carry the stigma of low ability.

Consequently, many secondary school students, despite their ability, will not expend the effort needed to achieve their potential. Underachievement can become a way of life.

Once students begin believing they have failed because they lack ability, they tend to lose hope for future success. They develop a pattern of academic hopelessness and stop trying. They see academic obstacles as insurmountable and devote less effort to learning.

Teachers who are alert to these beliefs in youngsters will keep their students motivated and on task. They will also slowly nudge their students toward the realism of judging themselves by performance. For example, teachers will set high expectations and insist that students put forth the effort required to meet the school's academic standards. They will make sure slower learners are rewarded for their progress and abler students are challenged according to their abilities.

19—MANAGING CLASSROOM TIME   WHAT WORKS

Research Finding: How much time students are actively engaged in learning contributes strongly to their achievement. The amount of time available for learning is determined by the instructional and management skills of the teacher and the priorities set by the school administration.

Comment: Teachers must not only know the subjects they teach; they must also be effective classroom managers. Studies of elementary school teachers have found that the amount of time the teachers actually used for instruction varied between 50 and 90 percent of the total school time available to them.

Effective time managers in the classroom do not waste valuable minutes on unimportant activities; they keep their students continuously and actively engaged. Good managers perform the following time-conserving functions:

- *planning class work:* choosing the content to be studied, scheduling time for presentation and study, and choosing those instructional activities (such as grouping, seatwork, or recitation) best suited to learning the material at hand
- *communicating goals:* setting and conveying expectations so students know what they are to do, what it will take to get a passing grade, and what the consequences of failure will be
- *regulating learning activities:* sequencing course content so knowledge builds on itself, pacing instruction so students are prepared for the next step, monitoring success rates so all students stay productively engaged regardless of how quickly they learn, and running an orderly, academically focused classroom that keeps wasted time and misbehavior to a minimum

When teachers carry out these functions successfully and supplement them with a well-designed and well-managed program of homework, they achieve three key goals:

- They capture students' attention.
- They make the best use of available learning time.
- They encourage academic achievement.

20—DIRECT INSTRUCTION   WHAT WORKS

Research Finding: When teachers explain exactly what students are expected to learn and demonstrate the steps needed to accomplish a particular academic task, students learn more.

Comment: The procedure stated above is called "direct instruction." It is based on the assumption that knowing how to learn may not come naturally to all students, especially to beginning and low-ability learners. Direct instruction takes children through learning steps systematically, helping them see both the purpose and the result of each step. In this way, children learn not only a lesson's content but also a method for learning that content.

The basic components of direct instruction are

- setting clear goals for students and making sure they understand those goals
- presenting a sequence of well-organized assignments
- giving students clear, concise explanations and illustrations of the subject matter
- asking frequent questions to see if children understand the work
- giving students frequent opportunities to practice what they have learned

Direct instruction does not mean repetition. It does mean leading students through a process and teaching them to use that process as a skill to master other academic tasks. Direct instruction has been particularly effective in teaching basic skills to young and disadvantaged children, as well as in helping older and higher ability students to master more complex materials and to develop independent study skills.

21—TUTORING   WHAT WORKS

Research Finding: Students tutoring other students can lead to improved academic achievement for both student and tutor, and to positive attitudes toward coursework.

Comment: Tutoring programs consistently raise the achievement of both the students receiving instruction and those providing it. Peer tutoring, when used as a supplement to regular classroom teaching, helps slow and underachieving students master their lessons and succeed in school. Preparing and giving the lessons also benefits the tutors themselves, because they learn more about the material they are teaching.

Of the tutoring programs that have been studied, the most effective include the following elements:

- highly structured and well-planned curricula and instructional methods
- instruction in basic content and skills (grades 1-3), especially in arithmetic
- a relatively short duration of instruction (a few weeks or months)

When these features were combined in the same program, the students being tutored not only learned more than they did without tutoring, they also developed a more positive attitude about what they were studying. Their tutors also learned more than students who did not tutor.

22—MEMORIZATION   WHAT WORKS

Research Finding: Memorizing can help students absorb and retain the factual information on which understanding and critical thought are based.

Comment: Most children at some time memorize multiplication tables, the correct spelling of words, historical dates, and passages of literature, such as the poetry of Robert Frost or the sonnets of Shakespeare. Memorizing simplifies the process of recalling information and allows its use to become automatic. Understanding and critical thought can then build on this base of knowledge and fact. Indeed, the more sophisticated mental operations of analysis, synthesis, and evaluation are impossible without rapid and accurate recall of bodies of specific knowledge.

Teachers can encourage students to develop memory skills by teaching highly structured and carefully sequenced lessons, with frequent reinforcement for correct answers. Young students, slow students, and students who lack background knowledge can benefit from such instruction.

In addition, teachers can teach mnemonics, that is, devices and techniques for improving memory. For example, the mnemonic "Every Good Boy Does Fine" has reminded generations of music students that E, G, B, D, and F are the notes to which the lines on a treble staff correspond. Mnemonics help students remember more information faster and retain it longer. Comprehension and retention are even greater when teachers and students connect the new information being memorized with previous knowledge.

23—QUESTIONING   WHAT WORKS

Research Finding: Student achievement rises when teachers ask questions that require students to apply, analyze, synthesize, and evaluate information in addition to simply recalling facts.

Comment: Even before Socrates, questioning was one of teaching's most common and most effective techniques. Some teachers ask hundreds of questions, especially when teaching science, geography, history, or literature.

Questions take different forms and place different demands on students. Some questions require only factual recall and do not provoke analysis. For example, of more than 61,000 questions found in the teacher guides, student workbooks, and tests for nine history textbooks, more than 95 percent were devoted to factual recall. This is not to say that questions meant to elicit facts are unimportant. Students need basic information to engage in higher level thinking processes and discussions. Such questions also promote class participation and provide a high success rate in answering questions correctly.

The difference between factual and thought-provoking questions is the difference between asking, "When did Lincoln deliver the Gettysburg Address?" and asking, "Why was Lincoln's Gettysburg Address an important speech?" Each kind of question has its place, but the second one intends that the student analyze the speech in terms of the issues of the Civil War.

Although both kinds of questions are important, students achieve more when teachers ask thought-provoking questions and insist on thoughtful answers. Students' answers may also improve if teachers wait longer for a response, giving students more time to think.

24—STUDY SKILLS   WHAT WORKS

Research Finding: The ways in which children study influence strongly how much they learn. Teachers can often help children develop better study skills.

Comment: Research has identified several study skills used by good students that can be taught to other students. Average students can learn how to use these skills. Low-ability students may need to be taught when, as well as how, to use them.

Here are some examples of sound study practices:

- Good students adjust the way they study according to several factors:
  - the demand of the material
  - the time available for studying
  - what they already know about the topic
  - the purpose and importance of the assignment
  - the standards they must meet
- Good students space learning sessions on a topic over time and do not cram or study the same topic continuously.
- Good students identify the main idea in new information, connect new material to what they already know, and draw inferences about its significance.
- Good students make sure their study methods are working properly by frequently appraising their own progress.

When low-ability and inexperienced students use these skills, they can learn more information and study more efficiently.

25—HOMEWORK: QUANTITY   WHAT WORKS

Research Finding: Student achievement rises significantly when teachers regularly assign homework and students conscientiously do it.

Comment: Extra studying helps children at all levels of ability. One research study reveals that when low-ability students do just 1 to 3 hours of homework a week, their grades are usually as high as those of average-ability students who do not do homework. Similarly, when average-ability students do 3 to 5 hours of homework a week, their grades usually equal those of high-ability students who do homework.

Homework boosts achievement, because the total time spent studying influences how much is learned. Low-achieving high school students study less than high achievers and do less homework. Time is not the only ingredient of learning, but without it little can be achieved.

Teachers, parents, and students determine how much, how useful, and how good the homework is. On average, American teachers say they assign about 10 hours of homework each week—about 2 hours per school day. But high school seniors report they spend only 4 to 5 hours a week doing homework, and 10 percent say they do none at all or have none assigned. In contrast, students in Japan spend about twice as much time studying outside school as American students.

26—HOMEWORK: QUALITY   WHAT WORKS

Research Finding: Well-designed homework assignments relate directly to class work and extend students' learning beyond the classroom. Homework is most useful when teachers carefully prepare the assignment, thoroughly explain it, and give prompt comments and criticism when the work is completed.

Comment: To make the most of what students learn from doing homework, teachers need to give the same care to preparing homework assignments as they give to classroom instruction. When teachers prepare written instructions and discuss homework assignments with students, they find their students take the homework more seriously than if the assignments are simply announced. Students are more willing to do homework when they believe it is useful, when teachers treat it as an integral part of instruction, when it is evaluated by the teacher, and when it counts as a part of the grade.

Assignments that require students to think, and are therefore more interesting, foster their desire to learn both in and out of school. Such activities include explaining what is seen or read in class; comparing, relating, and experimenting with ideas; and analyzing principles.

Effective homework assignments do not just supplement the classroom lesson; they also teach students to be independent learners. Homework gives students experience in following directions, making judgments and comparisons, raising additional questions for study, and developing responsibility and self-discipline.

27—ASSESSMENT   WHAT WORKS

Research Finding: Frequent and systematic monitoring of students' progress helps students, parents, teachers, administrators, and policy makers identify strengths and weaknesses in learning and instruction.

Comment: Teachers find out what students already know and what they still need to learn by assessing student work. They use various means, including essays, quizzes and tests, homework, classroom questions, standardized tests, and parents' comments. Teachers can use student errors on tests and in class as early warning signals to point out and correct learning problems before they worsen. Student motivation and achievement improve when teachers provide prompt feedback on assignments.

Students generally take two kinds of tests: classroom tests and standardized tests. Classroom tests help teachers find out if what they are teaching is being learned; thus these tests serve to evaluate both student and teacher. Standardized tests apply similar gauges to everyone in a specific grade level. By giving standardized tests, school districts can see how achievement progresses over time. Such tests also help schools find out how much of the curriculum is actually being learned. Standardized tests can also reveal problems in the curriculum itself. For example, a recent international mathematics test showed that U.S. students had encountered only 70 percent of what the test covered.

28—EFFECTIVE SCHOOLS   WHAT WORKS

Research Finding: The most important characteristics of effective schools are strong instructional leadership, a safe and orderly climate, school-wide emphasis on basic skills, high teacher expectations for student achievement, and continuous assessment of pupil progress.

Comment: One of the most important achievements of education research in the past 20 years has been identifying the factors that characterize effective schools, in particular the schools that have been especially successful in teaching basic skills to children from low-income families. Analysts first uncovered these characteristics when comparing the achievement levels of students from different urban schools. They labeled the schools with the highest achievement as "effective schools."

Schools with high student achievement and morale show certain characteristics:

- vigorous instructional leadership
- a principal who makes clear, consistent, and fair decisions
- an emphasis on discipline and a safe and orderly environment
- instructional practices that focus on basic skills and academic achievement
- collegiality among teachers in support of student achievement
- teachers with high expectations that all their students can and will learn
- frequent review of student progress

Effective schools are places where principals, teachers, students, and parents agree on the goals, methods, and content of schooling. They are united in recognizing the importance of a coherent curriculum, public recognition for students who succeed, promoting a sense of school pride, and protecting school time for learning.

29—DISCIPLINE   WHAT WORKS

Research Finding: Schools contribute to their students' academic achievement by establishing, communicating, and enforcing fair and consistent discipline policies.

Comment: For 16 of the past 17 years, the public has identified discipline as the most serious problem facing its schools. Effective discipline policies contribute to the academic atmosphere by emphasizing the importance of regular attendance, promptness, respect for teachers and academic work, and good conduct.

Behavior and academic success go together. In one recent survey, for example, high school sophomores who got "mostly As" had one-third as many absences or incidents of tardiness per semester as those who got "mostly Ds." The same students were twenty-five times more likely to have their homework done and seven times less likely to have been in trouble with the law. Good behavior as a sophomore led to better grades and higher achievement as a senior.

The discipline policies of most successful schools share these traits:

- Discipline policies are aimed at actual problems, not rumors.
- All members of the school community are involved in creating a policy that reflects community values and is adapted to the needs of the school.
- Misbehavior is defined. Because not everyone agrees on what behavior is undesirable, defining problems is the first step in solving them. Students must know what kinds of behavior are acceptable and what kinds are not.
- Discipline policies are consistently enforced. Students must know the consequences of misbehavior, and they must believe they will be treated fairly.
- A readable and well-designed handbook is often used to inform parents and students about the school's discipline policy.

30—UNEXCUSED ABSENCES   WHAT WORKS

Research Finding: Unexcused absences decrease when parents are promptly informed that their children are not attending school.

Comment: Absences are a major problem at all levels of school. Students who miss a lesson lose an opportunity to learn. Too many missed opportunities can result in failure, dropping out of school, or both. Research indicates parents want to hear promptly if their children have poor grades, are creating discipline problems, or have unexcused absences.

Schools have different ways of letting parents know when their children aren't in school. Some use staff members to check attendance records and phone the parents of absent students. Others have begun using automatic calling devices that leave a recorded message with parents. The usual message is a request to contact the school about the absence. These devices can be programmed to call back if no answer is received. Schools using such devices report substantial increases in attendance.

Good attendance in school is another example of the connection of time and learning. Just as homework amplifies learning, regular attendance exposes students to a greater amount of academic content and instruction. Students, of course, must concentrate on their lessons in order to benefit from attendance.

31—EFFECTIVE PRINCIPALS   WHAT WORKS

Research Finding: Successful principals establish policies that create an orderly environment and support effective instruction.

Comment: Effective principals have a vision of what a good school is and systematically strive to bring that vision to life in their schools. School improvement is their constant theme.

Principals scrutinize existing practices to ensure that all activities and procedures contribute to the quality of the time available for learning. They make sure teachers participate actively in this process. Effective principals, for example, make opportunities available for faculty to improve their own teaching and classroom management skills.

Good school leaders protect the school day for teaching and learning. They do this by keeping teachers' administrative chores and classroom interruptions to a minimum.

Effective principals visibly and actively support learning. Their practices create an orderly environment. Good principals make sure teachers have the necessary materials and the kind of assistance they need to teach well.

Effective principals also build morale in their teachers. They help teachers create a climate of achievement by encouraging new ideas; they also encourage teachers to help formulate school teaching policies and select textbooks. They try to develop community support for the school, its faculty, and its goals.

In summary, effective principals are experts at making sure time is available to learn and at ensuring that teachers and students make the best use of that time.

32—TEACHER SUPERVISION   WHAT WORKS

Research Finding: Teachers welcome professional suggestions about improving their work, but they rarely receive them.

Comment: When supervisors comment constructively on teachers' specific skills, they help teachers become more effective and improve teachers' morale. Yet, typically, a supervisor visits a teacher's classroom only once a year and makes only general comments about the teacher's performance. This relative lack of specific supervision contributes to low morale, teacher absenteeism, and high faculty turnover.

Supervision that strengthens instruction and improves teachers' morale has these elements:

- agreement between supervisor and teacher on the specific skills and practices that characterize effective teaching
- frequent observation by the supervisor to see if the teacher is using these skills and practices
- a meeting between supervisor and teacher to discuss the supervisor's impressions
- agreement by the supervisor and teacher on areas for improvement
- a specific plan for improvement, jointly constructed by teacher and supervisor

Principals who are good supervisors make themselves available to help teachers. They make teachers feel they can come for help without being branded failures.

33—RIGOROUS COURSES   WHAT WORKS

Research Finding: The stronger the emphasis on academic courses, the more advanced the subject matter; and the more rigorous the textbooks, the more high school students learn. Subjects that are learned mainly in school rather than at home, such as science and math, are most influenced by the number and kinds of courses taken.

Comment: Students often handicap their intellectual growth by avoiding difficult courses. In order to help young people make wise course choices, schools are increasingly requiring students to take courses that match their grade level and abilities; schools are also seeing to it that the materials used in those courses are intellectually challenging.

The more rigorous the course of study, the more a student achieves, within the limits of his capacity. Student achievement also depends on how much the school emphasizes a subject and the amount of time spent on it: the more time expended, the higher the achievement. Successful teachers encourage their students' best efforts.

WHAT WORKS IN SCHOOLS WORKS IN PROFESSIONAL FOOTBALL

It is easy to imagine the "33 plays" being applied on and off the field by an NFL coach. Although it is a game of strength and action, players and coaches repeatedly tell us professional football is "80 percent thinking" and mental preparation is ongoing.

The game takes 2 hours to play, and off-field practice scrimmages are only 2 to 3 hours a day. But the players and coaches constantly study and update the team playbook.

When applied in the classrooms of life—school, work, home, and football field—we are reminded of the power of praxis. Consider the story of James Harris. Who is he, and how did he make NFL history?

In 1969, as a member of the Buffalo Bills, James Harris succeeded Jack Kemp at quarterback. Harris became the first African-American ever to start a pro-football season opener at quarterback. What Jackie Robinson did for big league baseball, James Harris did for the NFL quarterback position. It was equally momentous.

At the time Harris noted, "There were some people who felt blacks weren't smart enough to play quarterback in the NFL. The pressure I felt in that first camp was just to survive."

Harris tried not to worry about it. He knew Coach John Rauch liked his stuff. But it wasn't all that clear that Harris could make it. He was a long shot, but his coach gave him the chance he needed.

Harris's career almost folded before he got rolling. He was an 8th round draft pick. He felt racism played a part in his low standing and almost quit right there and then. Harris was Player of the Year in black college football. Other professional teams had contacted him and indicated he would be drafted earlier if Harris would change his player position. It was at this point that he considered quitting.

He went home to clear the air. Harris talked with Eddie Robinson, his former coach at Grambling College—always a black college football powerhouse. He talked with his mother. Both convinced James Harris to keep going and turn pro. They knew that an opportunity like this might be a long time coming around again.

There had been black quarterbacks in the pro game before Harris, but always as a bench backup player. But James Harris was truly a pioneer. In 1975, playing for the L. A. Rams, James Harris led the team to the NFC championship. In the Pro Bowl that year, he was named the game's Most Valuable Player.

Such is the power of family, coaching, and mentoring.

CHAPTER 6

Sports Perspective and Leadership

THERE IS NO shortage of literature or advice about leadership. To read it all is impossible; to heed it all is probably foolish.

We are certain, however, there is one ingredient indispensable to the success of any enterprise: leadership. Peter Drucker put it succinctly by stating that if an enterprise fails to perform, we should not hire different workers but, instead, a new president. It is amazing how quickly a change at the top of certain organizations can change attitudes and behavior throughout the organization. This is especially evident in football.

- In professional football, the fans boo the coach out of town.
- In college football, the alumni "hang" the coach, figuratively.

Sports management involves skills and attitudes that can be defined, taught, and learned. Each member of the organization from players to coaches learns to manage his own work and that of teammates dependent upon him.

SPORTS DEFINES A *PROFESSIONAL* LEADER

It is precisely in answer to this question that the sports metaphor gains much of its power. Each fall, millions of Americans spend prime recreation hours (and hours away from work) on hard stadium seats or else glued to television sets and radios, watching or listening to *professional* football. They get a clear demonstration of leadership in action by observing the behavior of owners, coaches, and team leaders.

The key to understanding leadership centers on the word *professional* as it is used in sports. Why are the players, for example, called professionals? The quick and obvious answer is that they are not amateurs. While true, of course, the term *professional* in sports means far more than this: it means that they are the best at what they do – they get results.

Philadelphia Eagles Coach Denny Green gets results. He uses the theme of the week – a buzzword – to motivate his players. "One play at a time." "This is a game of the heart." "Let's build our house." "Focus." "Let's light the ignition and go up." "Stand up for what you believe." "It's there for the taking." By the end of the week, the word is burned into the player's mind.

They are not called professionals because they complete some prescribed course of instruction, or graduate from the right college, or even accumulate a specified number of years of experience. They are not professionals because they hold a degree or a certificate or a license to practice. In sports, in stark contrast to leadership in bureaucratic and hierarchical organizations (e.g., government, business, and schools), leaders are professionals for one and only one reason. It is their ability to perform what is required to get the intended results.

> "In football, winning isn't everything—it's the only thing."—Vince Lombardi

It is common to describe doctors, lawyers, engineers, architects, administrators, teachers, and others with similar vocations as professionals because they have met certain requirements of study and practice. It is assumed that a person who meets professional standards holds the ability to competently perform their specialization. This may or may not be true. The proof, using the sports perspective, can only be in whether they achieve the intended results, or at least carry out the position requirements in an authoritative way designated as "best practice."

The professional, who is fated to lead the complex changes demanded by the transformation from one economic era to another, must be the one whose chief characteristic is that of a leader in professional sports. In schools, academic qualifications and experience are necessary but not sufficient – true leadership centers on excellent performance.

Professional leadership precisely revolves around setting goals and the efforts to achieve them. Goal seeking is the executive's foremost activity.

For centuries, people with seemingly mysterious qualities of leadership have appeared in society. Popular opinion has held that such people are born not made. To be sure, there are innate characteristics that make some more qualified than others, but there is little doubt that any reasonably intelligent person can learn what it takes to be a competent leader. The sports perspective highlights the necessary qualities.

THE SPORTS METAPHOR AND CHANGE

Through professional sports, we are able to observe the impact of gradual and rapid change as it affects the system.

Football was first played in America, albeit in a crude form, by the Puritans in the early 1600s. Over the next 250 years, nothing much happened to football. In fact, Harvard and Yale abolished the game in 1860 because it was felt to be injurious to health.

The first U.S. football team organized to play under adopted rules (intended to civilize the sport) was organized in 1862.

The game or sport that emerges over time results from subtle and mostly planned changes. But, it is the deep and turbulent event that causes the playbook to be altered, that governs the actual playing of the game, and that changes the game forever. For instance:

- Soccer started out as entirely a kicking game. Over time, it took on many of the characteristics of what we now know as rugby. In 1823, William Webb Ellis decided to catch a kick and run it back the length of the field for a score, to the total amazement of the other team. Rugby was changed by that unorthodox behavior forever.
- By 1870, Harvard introduced a new rule to soccer allowing a player, under certain circumstances, to grab the ball and run with it. Again, a new paradigm was added and the foundation of a new game was formed.
- Amos Alonzo Stagg, who also invented the playbook, was quick to take advantage of rule changes. When the forward pass became legal to throw (underhand) in 1906, Stagg reportedly came up with sixty-four pass plays!
- The events of November 1, 1913, are legendary in football. Notre Dame upset West Point 35–13, all with *overhand* forward passes. Unknown to the Army cadets, two skinny kids, who were also roommates, Gus Dorias and Knute Rockne, spent the

previous summer between working hours practicing throwing forward passes baseball style, then running imaginary dodge patterns on the beach. Football hasn't been the same since.

- After World War II, football saw another turbulent change. The T-formation brought with it a new variation—the quarterback now took the ball directly out of the hands of the center. In an instant, the traditional single-wing and double-wing offensive formations were all but abandoned. The playbook had to be quickly rewritten!

SELECTION AND DEVELOPMENT OF INDIVIDUALS

In all sports, rules, boundaries, teams, referees, and leagues are established as a form of controlled reality. In the professional National Football League (NFL), distinct identities are created (e.g., Bears, Jets, Jaguars, Lions, Panthers, Rams, Giants). College football has a long tradition and is similarly focused (e.g., Fighting Irish, Hurricanes, Gators, Seminoles, Wolverines). With all sports, but especially with football, we craft a new form of reality—what has come to be called in the Information Age a *virtual reality*.

The evolution of U.S. sports has been marked by unorthodox and convulsive change events. Though now quite familiar to players and fans, these and other turning points have forged the kinds of players, game plans, and playbook now used. For example:

- A college front line averaging 300 pounds is no longer that unusual. Huge players, some of the largest human specimens, now move with the quickness and agility once only possessed by a top ball carrier in Jim Thorpe's day.
- The "Hail Mary Pass" heaved more than half the length of a 100-yard field, once the last-ditch desperation play, is now more commonly witnessed coming from the strong arm of a professional quarterback.
- Field goals kicked from mid-field every game attest to the strength and training of today's kickers. A 63-yard field goal stands as the NFL record.

American football, whether played on the sandlot, in high school, at college, or in the NFL has evolved into a game of skill, balanced with a player's physical abilities. It takes a bright mind and quick reflexes. A specific player may not necessarily be the biggest, fastest, or strongest person for a particular position, but he must be grounded in the solid basics of the sport – stance, blocking, tackling, running, passing, kicking. And those basics must be learned from the beginning with a striving for continuous improvement. Only by continuing to push himself beyond the basics to mastery will he arrive at a point where he feels secure for himself, for his position, and for his team.

ADJUSTING TO TODAY'S BALL PLAYER

For better or worse, the coach is three people: teacher, parent, and friend.

> "I don't want to pat myself on the back, but I never wanted to be just a football coach. It's important that the faculty understand that I think football has a place in the university, and that the tail's not wagging the dog."—Penn State Coach Joe Paterno (over *90 percent* of his players earn diplomas)

As a teacher, the coach must take the time and patience to educate these strong and virile young men, not only in the physical skills of the game but also in the mental aspects.

Next, as a parent figure, the coach is the one the player responds to when he fumbles the ball or tosses an intercepted pass. After every play, the players look to the coach for feedback (approval and positive body language). Denied this component, the player will soon become confused, disappointed, and unproductive.

Lastly, ball players eventually grow up to be adults. It's especially gratifying when ball players acknowledge their coach (or a teacher or manager) as a friend in the bigger game of life. This, too, is a vital part of the coaching, teaching, and mentoring process.

COACHES AS TEACHERS

> "Football is a game of errors. The team that makes the fewest errors in a game usually wins."—Paul Brown, legendary coach of the Cleveland Browns and playbook expert

Football has a large assortment of coaches: line, kicking, backfield and special team coaches. They constantly revisit the fundamentals to ensure team balance. They look for breakthroughs. Development coaches are specialists. They teach the art of finding breakthrough ideas. They also target control. In this coaching scenario, practical development and achievement are seamless.

If players are concerned about their assignments, they'll have a tendency to hold back. They need to be so familiar with the playbook and their assignments that when the game starts, they're running on autopilot, such as each of us experiences when we drive a car. When players are not distracted, they can let go and do what the job calls for.

Instruction, as coaches actually perform the role, is orderly and systematic. Its most important feature is that it must lead to demonstrated learning. To the coach, instruction has a central purpose: improving learning—learning focused on specific results.

There is a significant difference in sports among the administrative and content (curricular) decisions a coach makes and those he makes that deal with instruction. Administrative and content decisions are large; they emphasize *what* to do. The instructional decisions are narrow; they deal with *how* to implement the other decisions.

For instruction, the coach asks himself and others, "How best can we assure learning?" *How* decisions cause a careful search of the available praxis—the storehouse of good practice for results. *How* decisions summon experimentation and try-out to see if they actually work. Experimentation, feedback, and empirical evidence are the essence of good coaching in the improvement of individual player and team performance. They are also the heart of instruction.

If it became standard practice for educators to play a similar role in carrying out administrative and curricular decisions, it would certainly sharpen educational decision making and vastly improve instruction.

There are other benefits of *how* decisions. *How* decisions bolstered by try-out and empirical evidence lead to an improved professional praxis—an inventory of authoritative practices and tools for getting intended results. *Praxis makes perfect* goes along with the familiar *practice makes perfect*. Instruction using (1) authoritative practices, (2) conclusive principles, and (3) tools of professional praxis is a reproducible, researchable, and essentially and ideally a self-improving process.

This orderliness may be conveyed by an individual coach or the orderliness may be built into instructional settings, materials, and learning environments without the coach needing to be physically present. Regardless of the mode of presentation, when the process is called coaching, it is clearly the major form of instruction.

TEACHERS AS COACHES: THE EXECUTIVE ROLE

Effective teaching requires the same set of executive skills as coaching in football. Teachers must be helped to define and perfect these skills to increase their effectiveness in providing winning seasons. Why is this true?

Classrooms are like workplaces. Witness the common use of such terms as schoolwork, homework, and class work. They are like the practice playing field workplace in football. No glitz, no glamour, no bands, no pretty cheerleaders. These workplaces are complex and dynamic; they require management by an executive of considerable talent.

To be sure, teachers are rarely thought of as executives — indeed, they are, in terms of collective bargaining, defined as labor. But the reality of their new role is quite different from that of labor in a passing Industrial Age economy. The recognition of their role as leaders, coaches, and mentors in the Era 3 economy will help achieve long-neglected pay parity with responsibility and elevate the prestige of the profession, which is desperately needed. At the same time, implementing Era 3 standards will make teachers more effective in achieving intended student learning.

After thinking about the role of a football coach, the parallel between the behavior of these executives and the skills needed to run a public school classroom seem more obvious. Consider only the following four decisions all teachers must make:

(*1*) Choosing content
(*2*) Scheduling time
(*3*) Forming groups
(*4*) Choosing classroom and home-related activities

Further, they must communicate goals and purposes, regulate the activities of the workplace through pacing the learners, sequencing events, running an orderly and focused "game," preventing and controlling behavior problems, planning the work, creating the right "climate" for the work, inducting new "players" into the workplace, hooking the work in their workplace to other units in the school and to the system, supervising and working with other people including volunteers, motivating, and evaluating the performance of students and products.

GOAL POSTS FOR TEACHERS

Zen, as well as football, teaches that no one can stay the course without conscientious guidance from a skilled teacher and coach. As a player or a student, one has to overcome past inhibitions before successfully penetrating into the spirit of change.

Even if a pupil or player does not grasp the true significance of mastering a task, he or she can at least be helped to understand why some learning cannot be fun in itself like a sport or a gymnastic exercise. He or she must come to learn why the technically learnable part of the task must be practiced to the point of excess. If everything depends on the player or student becoming automatic and self-effacing in the event, then its outward realization must also occur automatically, in no further need of the controlling or reflecting intelligence. The student or player gives him- or herself over completely to the task.

In 1976, Tampa Bay became the first team in NFL history to finish a season 0–14. But Coach John McKay, who had won four national collegiate championships at USC, went on to win two NFC Central Division titles.

One of the many young prospects who yearned for a spot on the team was a rookie kicker named Pete Ryjecki. Foolishly, the naive lad told a reporter that he got really nervous when the coach watched him kicking. Coach McKay, after being told of the remark, sent Ryjecki a message reminding him that he planned to attend all the games.

It is this mastery of form that Japanese instruction through *kaizen* seeks to inspire. Practice, repetition, and repetition of the repeated with ever-increasing intensity are its distinctive features for long stretches. The football coach drills and re-drills his players until they run on auto-pilot.

Demonstration, example, imitation, and intuition are the fundamental relationship of teacher to pupil, of coach to player.

The teacher-pupil relationship has to be rekindled as a basic commitment of life. It presupposes, on the part of the teacher and coach, a high responsibility that far exceeds the scope of professional duties.

Nothing more is required of the pupil or player at first than that he or she should conscientiously copy what the teacher demonstrates. The teacher and coach look past blundering efforts, guide once again, and wait patiently for full growth.

STAFFING FOR RESULTS

Professional leadership literally revolves around the establishment of goals and the efforts to achieve them. Goal seeking is the leader's most important activity.

A major contribution of the sports metaphor to the success of any organization is the time, effort, and creativity used in finding and placing its people. The ability to choose the right person for each job is clearly one of the most important characteristics of the professional leader.

If our society would pick leaders with as much care and intelligence as the National Football League teams pick their quarterbacks, the benefits to society might be much greater than most people imagine.

THE FREE AGENT: NEW MODEL OF ECONOMIC BEHAVIOR

To succeed in today's fiercely competitive economy, Americans need both a collaborative and an individualistic "personalized" perspective (what we call *coopetition*). A key aspect of the sports perspective – the free agent – supplies some important aspects of that perspective.

The odds are better than 50–50 that if you are still employed in part of the Industrial Age economy, your job will disappear, no matter how many years of loyal service you've put in. There's nothing very abstract about what companies and the evening news call downsizing. This nicer sounding word than "firing" often translates into loss of self-esteem, sleepless nights, dramatic impacts on the family budget, marital stress, and stress-related illness. It has transformed many into pounding the pavement for work, writing resumes, waiting for phone calls that seldom come, and a reappraisal of one's personal package of skills.

In the world of professional sports, free agents are players who negotiate their contracts as individuals, rather than as part of a team. The first free agent was Curt Flood who, in 1969, when told he was being traded to the Philadelphia Phillies by his then team the St. Louis Cardinals, became a "no-show." Though Flood subsequently lost his anti-trust suit demanding freedom of choice, only 6 years later a federal arbitrator ruled in favor of free agency.

According to *American Demographics* (AD) (1993), "Today there are more free agents *off* the playing fields than on them." In 1940, only 11 percent of women and 20 percent of men agreed with the statement, "I am an important person." By 1990, two-thirds of women and 62 percent of men agreed. To succeed in today's fiercely competitive economy, Americans need an individualistic "personalized" perspective.

> Those who sit back and wait for someone to look out for them—be it spouse, an employer, or government—will end up on the sidelines. Only those who actively pursue their own interests by going to college, developing a specialty and marketing themselves to employers can hope to achieve prosperity.—*American Demographics* (1993)

Free agency has changed the dynamics of the NFL game, because the development of a system of football—the cooperative interaction between players over a period of years—is lost in a sense. Free agency gives a coach the chance to go out and improve his team without waiting for the next draft. "You rent the player—then you're married to that guy," said one coach. The coach is expected to win now, and there isn't time to develop players properly with frequent player changes.

In 1996, the NFL announced that 474 players were free agents who can negotiate with all 30 teams. Among that group of free agents were six players designated that year as franchise players and three who were named as transition players. One player was designated as exclusive franchise player prohibiting him from negotiating with another club.

Each NFL team was permitted to designate one of its players who would otherwise be an unrestricted free agent as a franchise player. The club that designates a franchise player must automatically offer the player a 1-year contract, averaging the five highest prior years' salaries at his position. A franchise player could still sign with another team, but that is highly unlikely since his original team would receive two first-round draft picks if he were sent elsewhere.

> "The strength of the league over its years has been the unity of its clubs. When NFL club presidents have been motivated to accomplish a goal for the overall good of the league, they have settled for nothing short of that mark. This motivation on the part of each individual club—to strive for that which benefits the entire league—has enabled the NFL to attain the measured success it has in the sports and entertainment field."—Pete Rozelle, former NFL commissioner

What is the practical result of all of this seemingly well-organized mayhem? First, it has resulted in players receiving the highest possible contracts for their specialized accomplishments in a very competitive sport. Second, it has equalized team play around the NFL in a manner that could not have been achieved under any other scenario. In 1995, their first season, the expansion Jacksonville Jaguars won only four games and also came within minutes and a point or two of winning four others. They beat the legendary Pittsburgh Steelers who later went on to play the Dallas Cowboys to a draw for three quarters before succumbing to the winner of Super Bowl XXX. The following year the expansion Carolina Panthers and the Jacksonville Jaguars each reached the playoff finals in their respective conferences. A mature form of simultaneous intra-league cooperation and competition—coopetition—and the free agent had leveled the NFL playing field and brought forth the reality of an old NFL adage, "that any team can beat any other team on a given day."

Viewed in terms of NFL football, a player may agree to stay with his current team for a stipulated period, protecting the team against losing the player, but the player will expect to be compensated for giving up his chance of moving to a better deal if one comes up. Deion Sanders moved in successive seasons from the Atlanta Falcons to the San Francisco 49ers to where he is under restricted contract with the Dallas Cowboys. He negotiated a whopping $25 million contract, but the Cowboys are protected for the term of the agreement. From the coach's point-of-view, it's great to pick up a star player, but it is a challenge to make eleven guys, who keep changing, into a winning team.

THE GAME KEEPS CHANGING

Football is a game of short bursts of activity called plays. If you execute the plays well, you move down the field and eventually score. Large-scale firms like Xerox, Ford, and AT&T score often and thrive.

Basketball is a game of speed. Speed and agility is what matters. Microsoft, Intel, and Compaq computers thrive. In the world of electronic communications, the fastest companies flourish.

The game has once again been redefined. Industry after industry has fallen victim to a fast-moving global economy. Innovative newcomers from all over the world preempt old and traditional practices. Several factors have contributed to new rules of the game:

(1) Customers are now more sophisticated. Access to information allows them to learn the meaning of value.

(2) The competitive playing field has expanded with lots of new global players – many using the work force of underdeveloped nations to produce.

(3) Advances in technologies have made substitution easier. There is now more cross-category competition (e.g., substituting plastics for copper).

(4) Low-cost information has increased outsourcing, thus lowering the competitive barriers to entry.

(5) New global competitors have easier access to capital – physical, financial, and human capital.

THE SPEED OF CHANGE DOUBLES AGAIN

The speed of changes such as these keep challenging the old rules. Long held beliefs about how to play the game have been uprooted. Execution and speed are more important than ever. But, neither is sufficient without knowledge. It raises new questions for each worker:

- Where will my value to a job or an employer come from?
- What competencies do I need to make the team? To stay on the team?
- What moves do I need to make to be ready for the next opportunity?

There are always winners and losers in the process of change. In each transition, the trauma of change is the trauma of how to change. When you learn to play a sport, you start by becoming acquainted with the positions on the team. You learn how the players are deployed straight out of the playbook. You learn how each position offsets an opposing position. You pick up some basic moves, simple actions (to create an opening, to lay a trap, to look for opportunities to get on the scoreboard). Your competence comes from knowing the rules and applying the playbook.

LEARNING PATTERNS

Learning to play a sport to win also means gaining the ability to see and understand patterns quickly. Every team's playbook, whether in football, basketball, baseball, or hockey, spells out shifts, fakes, actions—all moves intended to gain the advantage. But playing the game well means becoming familiar with the patterns of winners, teams, and those players who have come from behind—Joe Montana and Joe Namath—as well as those who dominate a particular sport. Learning how to play the game well—any game—on a day-to-day basis calls for comparative analysis. This is called benchmarking, but more about that later.

By examining patterns, you see and come to understand how specific positions and plays lead to specific outcomes. By looking ahead and picturing the consequences of the action you are taking, you can identify and focus on the most important positions and the keys to successful play execution. These are the linchpins of your game and the result of building a playbook for the new competitive setting. One way of learning to recognize the winning patterns is to benchmark the game experiences of others—wins and losses.

POLYPERCEPTION—SCANNING "REALITY" THROUGH MULTIPLE LENSES

There is a natural tendency for individuals and groups to focus inward. The stages of market force changes, customer wants, and new global players are silent, subtle, and asymptomatic. As with the progression of many diseases, these changes and their impacts slowly creep in. By the time you feel any symptoms, the disease has spread beyond treatment.

New competitors are not always easy to spot, namely due to their diffuse nature (they operate from anywhere in the world) and their technical characteristics (the art of substituting the new for the old). They arise from areas within our peripheral vision but not from within our traditional areas of our ordinary vision. Are we blind-sided by the play or simply not sufficiently attuned to where the play is coming from?

> "The mental part of football is more difficult than the physical. Mental preparation never ends, whereas with the physical side you can be on the field an hour and a half or two hours, blow the whistle and you're done. But the mental part goes on and on—when you're eating, when you're sleeping, and when you're walking around."—Coach George Allen

WIDENING YOUR COMPETITIVE FIELD OF VISION

Customers do not exist in a vacuum. They exist within some defined context. And the customer's priorities are affected by a constantly expanding range of option plays. As with football, the selection of plays is determined by the expected action of competitors. In a fast-moving, information-rich, global economy, the ball moves quick and sure, but not always in the direction you might expect.

A winning play calls for shifting away from tunnel vision, which is largely a result of thinking in a traditional context, to effective peripheral vision. To anticipate your opponent's moves, whether it be labor supply, product, production, or new markets, calls for reviewing your playbook defensive strategy and counter movements for two major offensive plays:

(*1*) Global competition: Swiftly moving actions taking place on a global basis means stretching your thinking beyond the "traditional teams" of the old post World War II reconstruction league of Germany and Japan. The "expansion league" now includes the new free-market players that were formerly only considered as "minor league" teams: Taiwan, Singapore, South Korea, India, Mexico, Brazil, Spain, China, and the former Eastern European countries including Russia.

(2) Inter-Enterprise Partnering (Coopetition): A new form of team building has sprung up. It reflects the venture formation of enterprises, formerly nonexistent, combining two essential capital resources — human capital plus financial capital. It serves as the infrastructure support for team leaders with the ability to energize and motivate workers anywhere in the world to outperform their counterparts in large bureaucratic settings. It is an investment in the many forthcoming championship seasons to be played during the information era. This affects the output of U.S. industry and its workers, the match between the output of schools and workplace needs, and the nation's future standard of living.

OLD HABITS DIE HARD

The symptoms and diagnoses of bureaucratic institutions, schools, government, and business have been studied and written about ad nauseam. Why then do the cures and preventative medicine remain almost constant? If a football or basketball or ice hockey or any sports team had multi-fold losing seasons, how long would it continue until corrective actions turned it around?

The first job of coping with consecutive losing seasons — a steady losing streak — is to erase a "losing" mindset. A good place to start is with that old chestnut encased in the institutional memory — this is the way we have always done things around here." That calls for leadership, a strong-willed leader with a vision: A Jimmy Johnson pacing the sidelines, or a Pat Riley at courtside, or a Tommy Lasorda in the dugout. Second, it requires building a playbook that lays out alternative actions (though not mutually exclusive actions) that point in the direction of top flight individual performance, consistent team performance, and a winning season one play at a time.

Beyond flexibility and global perspective, it calls for extending change actions and thinking deep into the organization so they prove more durable and define how the game is played; creating a team and team leadership that forces competitors to respond; sharpening each player's intuition to sense the next critical pinch; watching out for false moves that can cause a loss of ground leading to your opponents putting points on the scoreboard. Customer-focused satisfaction means making hundreds of small decisions, all of them right. The more right plays your team makes, the greater the margin for no errors.

Looking at the game films from past games for feedback and corrective action helps you analyze the key plays—those you want to avoid and those you would like to be able to repeat again. It helps you update your playbook series. Breaking old institutional mindset habits calls for four distinct actions:

(1) Use trial and error. It works in any field of learning.

(2) Study the games of winning teams. This leads to customer-focused thinking.

(3) Learn from past mistakes. Understand wrong moves; internalize the right ones.

(4) Perform controlled experiments. Look for new insight before breakthroughs.

The playbook calls for stamina of thought. Playing to win is an acquired skill. It is an unrelenting exercise to match patterns of play and individual performance to the countless amount of information already residing in your head. It is also exhilarating to learn and fun to play. In the games where the winning coaches have prevailed, the mistakes they have made as well as avoided are the new curriculum; they form the new syllabus for schools and business performance. Learning what they have done and how, and why, and then applying what you've learned is the highest level of satisfaction you can receive. You and your team's proficiency will improve with time and practice.

CHAPTER 7

What It Means to Compete in the Global Economy

THE GLOBAL ECONOMY has been developing for a long, long time. Prior to World War I, British trading companies provided tea and silk from China, opium from India, textiles from Britain, and spices from the Caribbean. British banks funded the building of U.S. and Australian railroads. At the time, technology existed to send information about prices from one edge of the developed world to another, forging a global commodities market, and shipping lines circled the globe carrying commerce.

The nature of the global economy has changed. Today, ideas are freely exchanged over the Internet and e-mail as easily as once discussed over a second cup of coffee. International trade and services have been surging in recent years.

We now live in a state of global interconnectedness. In the past, global trade was limited to a narrow, elite, and prosperous slice of the population. Today, a banker can move billions of dollars electronically. A software company can take orders in one country for delivery in another country. You drive to your shopping mall in a car comprised of parts assembled from all over the world to shop for consumer goods manufactured from around the world.

Winning in this new, fast-moving, global economy is a continuous series of plays—both offensive and defensive. There are lots of problems to be solved, new knowledge to be applied, many skills to be learned, new resources to be invested, and considerable profits to be made. In the new global economy, firms and individuals cooperate when there is a mutual need and share risks out of mutual commitment to common objectives.

In the new global economy, individuals, enterprises, communities, and nations have two choices: (1) they can compete by reducing costs, mostly in the form of lowering wages to workers or (2) by improving overall productivity, which includes effectiveness and quality. That's it. These are literally the *only* variables for choice. On this, there is general agreement.

If reducing costs through savings on labor is the chosen route to compete, the competition will mostly be with third-world nations, and the direction of American wages is predictable — it will be downward.

The advice from the economists: if we do not want to get poor, we must compete by thinking and working smarter, compete on the basis of effectiveness, quality, and efficiency — the full meaning of productivity.

To continue the American Dream, there is really only one choice: quality and productivity. In economic terms, it can be seen as a supply and demand decision. The question is, where do Americans want to fall on the new global labor supply curve? At what point on the demand curve can we maximize optimal performance and achieve the profit measure of success?

If the quality and productivity route is chosen — and there seems little incentive to take the other path — there are several key issues that must be squarely faced. First, there is increasing need for worker knowledge through higher-order thinking skills. Mind-power is the energy that fuels the quality/productivity choice. Always an important factor before, now it becomes the principal source of energy.

High-performance organizations are the engines that increase productivity. The quality of human resources — its people — determines how well an enterprise can be organized for high performance. In the NFL, it is the pragmatic application of human resources that fulfills its principal missions — sports entertainment and business.

The payoff for increases in human capital is greater than that in other forms. For instance, labor is roughly 70 percent of America's gross domestic product (GDP); capital is roughly 30 percent. Therefore,

- A 5 percent increase in capital per worker increases productivity by 1.5 percent ($.05 \times 30 = 1.5\%$).
- The same increase in labor skills — the human capital — boosts productivity by 3.5 percent ($.05 \times 70 = 3.5\%$).

With more than a twofold advantage distributed over more than twice the amount of GDP, it is clear that productivity and quality is the preferred choice and offers the greater potential payoff. Doing so successfully means *all* who work and serve in the U.S. economy must have the knowledge and higher-order thinking skills that are required. It is no longer realistic or doable for enterprises and workers to depend solely on the 25 percent who go to college and make up the backbone of our professional, technical, and managerial work force. These workers must especially continue to learn and to improve their knowledge-base.

In the America of the 1950s, 60 percent of all jobs required few skills beyond the willingness to work hard and show up on time. Many of these jobs, especially in the nation's booming, Industrial Age, mass-production economy, were good paying jobs. For the most part, they offered a secure financial future for high school graduates and dropouts alike (73 percent of manufacturing jobs in 1950 were unskilled). By the 1990s, however, only 35 percent of jobs in America were unskilled. The figure is expected to drop to as low as 15 percent by the turn of the century.

It is also clear that the information-based economy demands a different set of work skills than those traditionally achieved by the overwhelming majority of our work force. There is now consensus about the skills required for a world-class American work force, the ability

(1) To learn

(2) To think for oneself

(3) To make judgments

(4) To read and think analytically

(5) To communicate effectively

(6) To work well with others

(7) To take responsibility for oneself

"Most people think football is strictly a muscle game. In the pros, though, every club is loaded with so much power that sheer strength is canceled out. You've got to outsmart the other team to win, and that takes enormous concentration on details."—Frank Gifford, former N.Y. Giants halfback/end and sports broadcaster

The battles between computer software leader Microsoft, web-browser leader Netscape, AT&T, the "Baby Bells," and a host of Internet Service Providers (ISP) are devoid of labor in the traditional sense. The innovative genius of product managers, software developers, marketers, and technical service specialists is the competitive edge.

Contrast, if you will, the complexity of your selecting and the phone company providing myriad services today with when you were a kid. Soon, your local cable company will offer phone and high-speed computer access. Your neighborhood TV store already sells and installs satellite TV—an 18″ dish mounted outside of your residence so you can receive "cable-less sports and entertainment" from the heavens.

For the foreseeable future, what counts is the ability to attract, hold, and continually improve the capabilities of knowledge workers as well as providing a management environment that breeds further ingenuity and change. And, in such a world, an organization (whether global or neighborhood sized) will be competitive only so long as its workers can learn faster than either its present or emerging competitors. Since almost any product can be copied, in this race for new markets, only lifelong worker and organizational learning provides the competitive edge.

BERETTA FIREARMS—CASE STUDY OF SIX EPOCHS
(Adapted from the History of Beretta)

The Italian gun maker Beretta is a unique company to study, because it allows us to track the 500-year history of one firm. Beretta also provides a singularly unique perspective on the impact of technology on the work force, management fads, and eventually market changes over a very long period of time—all changes triggered by technological episodes that developed outside of the firm.

Reviewing this experience from such an unusually long view helps demonstrate the evolution of management thinking; how technology affected management behavior; how today's technology hastened the return to a modern form of product customization not seen or experienced since the guild craft era; the impact of advanced manufacturing processes; and, most importantly, *why*—the evolution and subsequent demand for a new type of knowledge worker. Given the central role played by war and guns, it is safe to say that Beretta has been a factor in global trade since the earth was perceived as flat.

At about the same time that Christopher Columbus, with his fleet of tiny ships, Nina, Pinta, and Santa Maria, stumbled upon the New World, Beretta, a family gunsmith firm was being founded. It was 1492, during what is defined by historians as the era of the Guild System.

Initially, all Beretta guns were handmade by master gun makers. There were no plans. The master used calipers, jigs, clamps, and files. An apprentice watched so as to learn the craft. All activities centered around *fit*. Parts were hand modified to fit tightly with other parts. As a result, every gun was a one-of-a-kind. In those days, parts were *not* interchangeable. These early instruments of war were crafted by highly skilled and trained workers, much the same as the early cabinet and clock-case makers.

In 1800, the Industrial Revolution instigated the English System of the then modern Era 2 production. The Industrial Age brought with it for the first time the development of new and uniform tools and universal fabrication, e.g., metal lathes. The system separated the production function from the processes used to make Beretta firearms.

In the 1880s, apprentices were taught proficiency on a particular tool, rather than on a particular product. An era of worker specialization was evolving that enabled process improvements to be made independently of product constraints.

Beretta introduced early mass production. Their workers were then expected to have fewer universal skills, but the worker needed to be trained to be more task specific and tool-centered. This uniformity led to fully interchangeable but also de-skilled workers. Such production systems became popular and widespread throughout industrial Europe and on to America.

The American System of production developed in the 1850s, and the Industrial Age here moved into a new phase. High-volume production of products with interchangeable parts became the order of the day. Driven by mechanization, the workers became interchangeable, but still viewed as only a by-product of production. In the American System, the Beretta product line was pared down to three models. Rigid production process and worker efficiencies became the rationale for avoiding product customization.

Then, Frederick W. Taylor came along. Taylor sought to refine the early Industrial Age production methods discussed in his 1911 book *The Principles of Scientific Management.* The Taylor Scientific Method, as it was known, sought to make labor as efficient as machine tools—specialized and interchangeable. Work was redesigned through time and motion studies. It used man-machine process interaction to determine the most efficient organization. Efficiencies and product shifts then allowed Beretta to increase its product catalog from three weapons to ten. Job responsibilities were broken down to specialty trained workers. Work discretion was replaced with Taylor's "one best way to perform the task." Management controlled all aspects of work, comparing performance to pre-set standards. His industrial methods have been overtaken by time and modern events, but one Taylor admonition still holds a ring of good advice for teachers and managers.

> This change can be brought about only gradually and through the presentation of many object-lessons to the workman, which together with the teaching which he receives, thoroughly convince him of the superiority of the new over the old way of doing the work. This change in the mental attitude of the workman imperatively demands time.—Frederick W. Taylor, *The Principles of Scientific Management* (1967 edition, p. 131)

By the end of World War II (1945), Statistical Process Control had come into widespread use. NATO (North Atlantic Treaty Organization) required M-1 rifle parts with tolerances calling for perfectly interchangeable parts. Beretta responded to this customer demand by building new manufacturing equipment for the task. Regular sampling was used for quality control, but only deviations were scrutinized. No best way to operate was yet found, because quality engineering occurred at the end of the production line while problem-solving teams monitored machine performance. The manufacturing process was not yet recognized as needing to be seamless.

By 1976, Beretta began to apply W. Edwards Deming's *Methods of Numerical Control*, then proven so successful in bringing the Japanese post-war "Economic Miracle." In Japan, *kaizen* is ingrained in the culture of a people dedicated to continuous improvement in all facets of life: product, production, and personal. To this day, the genius of Deming's methods lay in the fact that they were both a motivation and a natural extension of the way the Japanese see life.

Information processing could now be used to numerically control machines automatically and perform in sequence tasks that had previously taken multiple pieces of employment. With new forms of statistical control, it was now possible to exert a span of control five times greater, covering several machines at once. At the same time, the new standardized product demanded much better trained workers than at any time since the 18th century.

Another new era began at Beretta. New production equipment and new management methods allowed Beretta to bid a price one-half of that of their U.S. competitors. The transportability of numerical control programs enabled Beretta to meet the U.S. Army (the customer) stipulation of delivering from full U.S.-based production.

In the early 1980s, Americans were shocked to learn that the Beretta 9-mm Parabellum won the U.S. Army contract replacing the historic Colt-45 sidearm. The mainstay of the U.S. military for more than 150 years had fallen to a global competitor.

With numerical control, Beretta had now evolved from a user of information to an information-based corporation. Data to manufacture products were stored digitally on computers rather than on blueprints, dies, and molds. In 1987, computer-integrated manufacturing (CIM) became the norm at Beretta, linking together the entire company with computer networks to perform computer-aided design (CAD), engineering, and flexible manufacturing systems right on the factory floor. This process used

- a computer controlled team of semi-independent workstations connected by automated material handling systems of looped conveyors that carried pallets bearing individual work pieces
- supervisory computers that carried information about these work pieces, directed movements of materials and components through manufacturing process, and assigned priorities and queue
- information-driven machines that reacted to changing situations, loaded correct numerical programs in proper machines, and monitored results as occurred

The effect of CIM proved startling. First, there was a three-to-one jump in productivity. The Beretta factory floor was now down to thirty machines, which was the lowest in 150 years. Thirty people was the minimum staffing, fewer people than Beretta had employed at the end of the 17th century. Rework had fallen to zero. Staff positions—

knowledge-workers—now represented two-thirds of the Beretta work force.

At Beretta, manufacturing had now evolved into a service. Customized products are available to special market segments. In turn, this has raised the demands for highly skilled, knowledge-based workers at every level of the company.

For the first time since the Guild days, 300 years ago, Beretta is theoretically capable of creating numerous different products. Customization is almost an unlimited capability. And Guild Era craftsmanship, in a 21st century model, has returned. Beretta has come full circle.

FORMULA FOR LEVELING THE GLOBAL PLAYING FIELD

> Coopetition: The phenomenon of companies, located anywhere in the world, joining their competitors on a project-by-project basis. The products have sometimes been referred to as "Alliance Ware."

Economic textbooks may have difficulty embracing *coopetition* (cooperation and competition) with the same party. In 1994, the authors first began studying this phenomenon and, through workshop papers, developed a simple twelve-point playbook checklist to help ease the paradigm shift from the traditional either-or to the both-and to building an effective alliance:

(1) Build commitment from the outset. People make collaborations work.

(2) Devote time to the effort; otherwise skip it. All ventures require coaching.

(3) Get issues on the table early. Trust is an underpinning.

(4) Think win-win—you have to give up something to get something.

(5) File the legal contract—build understanding during the contractual process.

(6) Situations change; recognize your partner's problems. Be flexible.

(7) Define expectations and time frames. Encourage partners to do the same.

(*8*) Develop personal relationships; friendship helps overcome adversity.

(*9*) Prize different cultures. Work toward understanding them.

(*10*) Remember partner independence; recognize different interests; win-win.

(*11*) Get a strategic commitment; facts and risks on the table early; no surprises.

(*12*) Share the fruits of victory; celebrate success; share as would a family.

DOES COOPETITION WORK?

Sometimes yes, sometimes not. Coopetition is a mindset driven by the overriding objective that *mutual* success is the superior and most desirable result.

The NFL model is an example. Each week, the teams battle it out (compete) on the playing field trying to reach that championship season. The owners recognize the intrinsic value of their franchise, which only is as good as its support from the fans. It is the fan — the customer — who is king. The owners have crafted a system (cooperation) of teams, conferences, playoffs, player drafts, and free agents to level the competition. The sport provides a simulation of life and death warfare (competition). Each performance is seen by 60,000 to 80,000 fans in a multi-million dollar stadium as well as seen by millions each week on TV as games rotate on the sports networks (cooperation). It is all top draw entertainment. At its foundation is a big business, which has evolved through mutual need and trust as a model of coopetition.

Ford (U.S.) and Mazda (Japan) have had a long and profitable international venture since 1979. For Ford, the payoff has come partly in design and sales. While in 1992 the auto industry and the White House teamed to break down Japan's closed doors to U.S. car and auto parts sales, Ford had already been the best-selling foreign nameplate in Japan for several years, being sold through a jointly owned dealer network with Mazda.

In 1985, Ford built its new plant in Hermosillo, Mexico, using the successful Mazda Hofu (Japan) factory as a model (cooperation). A vastly improved line of Ford cars and trucks were influenced and brought to market through joint styling and engineering. Ford-aided Mazda cars and trucks were also successfully introduced. Ford has also gone on to use the Mazda coopetition model to introduce a joint Nissan-designed mini-van—the Mercury Villager. The 1997 Ford and Mazda product changes reflected a unique blend of new thinking (cooperation). Ford went on to purchase a larger stake in Mazda, and their relationship continues to evolve, as would any marriage in its stage of growing older together. Today, Ford and Mazda dealerships stand near each other on most automobile merchandising rows where they battle it out for the customer's dollars (competition).

On the other hand, General Motors has had its ups and downs. GM sold its interests in Daewoo (S. Korea) and continues its relationship with Isuzu (Japan). Chrysler and Mitsubishi continue along a somewhat rocky road with some cross benefits being brought to market, especially in product design. Isuzu has expanded its truck production for the Honda and Acura badged U.S. sport utility vehicle market.

In the Information Age, coopetition takes on multiple dimensions. "It's increasingly important to be able to compete and cooperate at the same time, but that calls for a lot of maturity," writes Microsoft Chairman Bill Gates in *The Road Ahead* (1995). The almost head-spinning growth of Internet usage has brought forth innovative agreements. Netscape Communications, developer of the leading Internet browser software with an 85 percent market share, persuaded America Online (AOL) with more than 6 million subscribers to their proprietary service to license Navigator software. The Internet reportedly has 20 million users and is adding more every day.

AOL then turned around and signed a separate marketing pact with AT&T Corporation's new Internet access service. The nonexclusive agreement calls for AOL service to be sold with AT&T's new WorldNet service. Basically, AT&T will display on their screen the AOL icon, allowing instant user connection to AOL and at a special rate. Then, AT&T has gone on to negotiate a similar agreement with AOL chief rival CompuServe. If successful, AT&T would then become the point of entry to the Internet as well as offering access to a range of proprietary information services.

On another front, Microsoft entered into agreement with Hewlett Packard to jointly develop a Microsoft brand, low-cost PC for the consumer market, complete with streamlined Microsoft software suites.

Microsoft then turned to Intel and Direct TV Inc., to jointly allow PCs to receive video programming now available to homes with TV satellite dishes. Subscribers would have access to a new category of multimedia services.

THE ORACLE BUSINESS ALLIANCE PROGRAM: MODEL FOR SUCCESS

Oracle's Business Alliance Program (BAP) fosters expanding relationships with leading information technology companies around the world to provide mutual customers with a broad range of products and services. More than 5,000 participants, including software developers, hardware vendors, distributors and re-sellers, consultants, and systems integrators, currently offer more than 3,500 products and services that support Oracle technology.

Oracle has crafted alliances of different characteristics depending on partner capabilities. Among the programs are Oracle Alliances with

- independent software vendors and hardware and operating system providers
- professional services and systems integration providers
- value-added distributors, and education and training services providers

Oracle's business alliance support programs are equally impressive, including a full array of services for members such as

- technical support, benchmarking services, user and developer conferences
- technical training, global sales support, and joint market development
- catalogues, WWW, and publications, business alliance conferences
- consistent worldwide business practices, flexible financing, and contracts

The BAP helps promote sales opportunities, globally, for companies that provide Oracle-based products and services. Of the 5,000 companies that have already joined the BAP, many are leaders in their own markets. Oracle offers advanced technology and products and is a global market leader. Oracle brings value-added propellant to an alliance engine to help partners increase market share and improve their bottom line.

Has Oracle's alliance program delivered real results for its members? "Yes," according to Ray Lane, President of Oracle Worldwide Operations. "In 1993, indirect sales accounted for only 11% of Oracle's license revenue. In 1995, that number grew to over 30% of our $1.6 billion-plus license revenue." Lane attributes this significant jump directly to the success of the Business Alliance Program. Oracle has targeted the goal of realizing more than 50 percent of its revenue through business alliances by the end of 1997.

All too often, the partners duplicate resources rather than making them mesh. Avoiding duplication and redundancy, both hallmarks of a management bureaucracy, usually signals management's real commitment to working together. "The concern is always there that one party will benefit unfairly from what you're about to do," said David Gunderson, liaison between Ford and Mazda (*Business Week,* February 10, 1992).

THE INFORMATION AGE: NEW TECHNOLOGY FOR NEW TIMES

Changes in technology have taken place over time. Some have been the drivers of dramatic transformations in our work and personal lives. The shift to the Industrial Age was clearly one of these transformations. The invention of the printing press combined with the invention of paper is another. Suddenly, the ability to easily share information and ideas was vastly expanded. Books of Greek philosophy were printed in one country and distributed throughout Europe. The ideas of the Reformation were quickly and widely spread through pamphlets.

Today, we are moving through a major transformation as we trek from the Industrial Age toward the new Information Age. The best technological evidence of this major change is the Internet and World Wide Web. This combination will undoubtedly have as great an impact or a greater impact on our lives as the printing press and paper. This vigorous pair allows us to share information and ideas, globally, as never conceived of before. It creates a more level playing field, global market opportunities, and a virtual work force. It allows people to live and work in almost any lifestyle they prefer. This shift will have social, economic, and political implications more powerful than the shift from the Agricultural to the Industrial Age, and it will happen much more quickly.

Many critically important rules are changing—intellectual property rights, copyrights, and availability of information. This information revolution is widely recognized, and there is no shortage of those commenting upon these events including a variety of leading thinkers, economists, futurists, academicians, and technologists.

INTER-ENTERPRISE COLLABORATION

Once hard and fast distinctions between competitors, customers, and suppliers have given way to new circumstances and situations. The spawning of coopetition is part cooperator/collaborator and part competitor. With unprecedented economic shift, competitive boundaries are continuously moving and converging (witness, for example, the birth of the new "infotainment" industry). Successfully running new play patterns through this emerging chaos requires enterprise to continually reevaluate where and what type of "focused competencies" it needs to get to be competitive. Vexing questions are raised:

- What types of inter-enterprise relationships need to be forged in response to escalating market changes?
- How will your company need to manage new alliances?
- What role will outsourcing play?
- How will your company determine with whom to team in the information-rich, global marketplace?

In building a playbook series for schools, you must similarly answer how will educators prepare students to perform, persist, and prosper for themselves and for enterprise in such a rapidly changing economic climate?

The richness of NFL sports provides an abundant example.

- *NFL Math 96* offers an exciting CD-ROM math program for kids 8 to 12. Math problems are based on official NFL statistics, e.g., three touchdowns with successful extra-point attempts plus three field goals equals 30 points.

- The *Jacksonville Times-Union* offers teachers of grades 5 through 8 *Tackle Geography*. At the beginning of football season, students receive their own *Tackle Geography* workbook containing lessons in compass direction, latitude, longitude, weather, distance, and unique area characteristics. Using the sports section each Monday through the NFL season, these students travel with the NFL teams to game destinations while they have fun learning geography.

ACTION PLANS FOR THE CLASSROOM
(adapted from Coach George Allen, 1990)

1. *Keep 'em loose* — No one should overestimate the value of a specific classroom lesson plan. One of the reasons that consistently winning ball teams are successful is that they operate from an organized routine and do not deviate from it. The players (or students) know what to expect. Knowing what to expect allows the player (student) to come prepared.

However, some flexibility is always necessary, because an opportunity may arise that will heighten student interest. Like football athletes, telling students that an assignment is difficult and will require total dedication is a way of stimulating curiosity. The tougher tasks automatically generate curiosity. They may complain, but they will react more quickly than usual.

Keep 'em loose. No coach wants his team to fall into the trap of boredom or a predictable pattern, because the real game, on and off the playing field, is anything but predictable. Football and global competition have more in common than even we at first suspected. Periodically changing the furniture around in the classroom can help change the atmosphere. Move the desks to different locations. Try it. It will keep students alert and let them know you are looking for ways to improve. The goal is twofold:

- to strive to be more efficient
- to stir the interest of the players (students)

2. *Lead the class with "class"* — Here's a list for winning classroom results:

- Always start on time.

- Maintain an enthusiastic approach.
- Keep a business-like style.
- Keep a sense of humor.
- Keep moving, quickly and efficiently.
- Use props: charts, films, visuals.
- Keep a clean blackboard.
- Print or write legibly.
- Keep asking questions to keep the students on their toes.
- At the end of class, review what's on tap for the next session.

Good teachers are hard to come by, and we should do everything we can to encourage them to continue their efforts in the classroom.

3. *Teaching is show business* — Prepare your notes the night before, if not earlier. When you meet with a class every day, it requires constant research and preparation. To be on top of the situation

- Organize materials so that you know exactly what you want to cover each day.
- Outline the important points that need to be stressed during the presentation.
- Practice delivery, even your voice inflection, to blot out mistakes and rambling.
- Reduce the amount of talking by using charts, slides, and written assignments.
- Allow flexibility to allow students to take part. Flexibility in the classroom as on the field is essential.

4. *Think of it as customer-relations* — There is never enough time for parents and teachers to visit together, so we need to develop some good service habits in dealing with the customer:

- Practice empathy. Parents want teachers to like their kids. Even though at times one of the students may cause trouble, true empathy allows a teacher to be more successful.
- Develop a note or card or short letter system to let parents know how the students are doing in the classroom. Report card time isn't enough. Stay in touch, even with only a short "e-mail type" message; it goes a long way in building customer support and mutual satisfaction.
- Be professional, all of the time. Students know the difference

between real and ersatz discipline. Establish the tone early. The student wants to know what the teacher demands, and this can be communicated effectively without words.

5. *Handling tough guys (and gals):*

- Find out what he or she wants.
- Find out what he or she rejects.
- Never criticize him or her in front of others.
- Give him or her private counseling to better understand.
- Be willing to compromise at the start.
- Be sincerely interested in helping the student.
- Be patient, and you will develop a leader.

SCOTLAND'S SILICON GLEN: CASE STUDY IN COOPETITION

Most of the world business press and TV talk shows have concentrated their focus on the competitive activities of Southeast Asia, more particularly Japan and company. But quietly and almost unnoticed, halfway around the world, the principles of coopetition are being played out in, for an American, an out of the way place. It offers yet another lesson in the magic of learning and earning.

Today, 10 percent of the world's PCs and 40 percent of Europe's PC market is held by the Scots. IBM, AT&T, Motorola, NEC, Adobe, HP, DEC, and Sun Microsystems all have built large facilities in an area of Scotland dubbed *Silicon Glen.*

Why? Scotland has—because of an outstanding school system—a highly skilled technical work force, an abundance of engineers, and a solid work ethic.

National Semiconductor (NSI) located its largest plant outside the U.S. in Scotland. NSI builds all of their analog chips here. Intel is their largest customer. Analog chips are widely used in audio equipment, air conditioning, fuel injection, anti-lock braking systems, computer hard drives, and mouses. In fact, there are more analog chips in the modern PC and MAC than digital chips.

In Scotland, there is a different work ethic, even among competitors who share facilities in the event of emergencies. It is not uncommon for one manufacturer to offer the use of their production lines to a competitor in times of emergency need.

NSI also picked Scotland for its worldwide training center. Here, workers are taught and learn the entire process—both strengths and weaknesses. NSI demonstrates the belief that those who learn faster remain ahead of their competitors.

IBM came to *Silicon Glen* for its new worldwide headquarters for displays, monitor, and manufacturing. All monitors must be adjusted for their physical location in relation to the earth's magnetic fields. Here, IBM has created a virtual world in order to properly calibrate monitors to work at the ship-to locations anywhere on the face of the globe.

More than three dozen firms got together and established *Glen Net,* an ISDN network that ties together all of the firms (friend or foe, supplier or competitor) in the Glen where they daily practice coopetition: cooperation among engineers in competing and supplying companies. One engineering manager was quoted as saying that design problems that used to take weeks or even months to resolve through meetings, fax, and missed phone calls are now cleared up in 5 minutes.

AT&T also chose Scotland as the place to develop its next generation of automatic teller machines (ATM). The new ATM is intended to be the last stop for paper in a paperless banking system—actually endorsing checks, doing the accounting, and completing all transactional events. For bank customers, it cuts waiting time; for the bank, it lowers costs.

COOPETITION AND A NEW VIEW OF CONTROL

As American management cautiously moves toward the inevitable growth in the number of coopetition agreements in a global marketplace, it needs to overcome the delusion that total control ensures the chance of success. Control does not necessarily lead to a better-managed enterprise. You cannot manage a global enterprise through muscle. In fact, this form of control is a last resort—it's what you fall back on when all else fails—when you are willing to risk demoralizing workers and managers.

Need for control is deeply rooted. Traditions of American enterprise, driven by legal and accounting rules, have taught generations of managers the incorrect arithmetic: that 51 percent equates with 100 percent and 49 percent with 0 percent. Fifty-one percent may buy you full legal control, but it is control of rapidly changing markets and globally-based customers, about which you may know little.

GENERAL CUSTER'S PLANS AFTER LITTLE BIG HORN

Pat Riley, former coach of the N.Y. Knicks basketball team, in his book *The Winner Within,* relates a not often told story of General George Armstrong Custer who, as history has taught us, seriously underestimated his rivals. Apparently, General Custer had big plans to gain the 1876 Democratic nomination for President of the United States. Custer had planned to telegraph ahead to St. Louis just as soon as he and his men dispensed with Chief Sitting Bull at Little Big Horn, South Dakota. As a military hero, Custer felt he could whip the Republican candidate handily. Well, we all know what happened next.

The key point to remember is, whether it be in sports or war or global business, one cannot ever underestimate the strength or resourcefulness of the opponent. American workers, managers, and leaders may have an unfortunate tendency to believe that the so-called "American Century" automatically imbued us with the strength and power to dominate the 21st century. Nothing could be further from the reality of the present situation. Our leaders, educators, and students have their work cut out for them now, more so than ever.

Coopetition then surfaces as the only reasonable approach to holding your own in the new and brutally competitive, yet necessarily collaborative, global economy. Coopetition requires loyalty among competitors, trust, craftsmanship, and cooperation, as well as power sharing among employees.

THE QUALITY PERSPECTIVE

Webster's New World Dictionary of the American Language defines quality as "the degree of excellence which a thing possesses." It defines excellence as "the fact or condition of excelling; superiority; surpassing goodness, merit." Most people support this notion of quality—linking the concept with the idea of being best either as a product or a service. There is a problem with this notion of quality, and it is a severe one in this age of transition between economies.

The problem of assuming that quality is simply "doing well whatever it is that you do best" is shown by the following example. A manufacturer of radios produces a premium, top-of-the-line, vacuum tube radio for home use. The radio case is finely crafted, the vacuum tubes are state-of-the-art, the price is reasonable, and the radio works like a gem. Despite the quality of the product — it meets the conventional notion of quality — the producer goes out of business because of a lack of sales. The product, even though it is of the highest quality as determined by the producer, does not meet the desires of the customer.

> New Economy Quality Fact #1: It is no longer profitable to ignore customer need as a basic dimension of quality.

> New Economy Quality Fact #2: Quality is defined by whether the customer's expectations and requirements are met or exceeded time after time—it is the product's or services' *fitness for use*.

We have now the definition of quality that best meets the demands of the new economy: *quality is fitness for use as judged by the user — the customer or client.*

Quality improvement, experts agree, requires a change in perspective — a change in the culture itself of an organization or enterprise. First, since the customer is now truly king or queen, the organization must create new partnerships with the employees; they, after all, are the direct link with the customer. Second, the new perspective implies that the *system,* not solely the employee, is viewed as the major cause of quality problems. These two shifts, driven by the new definition of quality, require two essential actions:

(1) *Create new partnerships with employees:* Partnerships promote the sense of ownership so vital in fostering a real commitment to the new understanding of quality. Employees who have ownership in their work see themselves as responsible for its quality.

(2) *The system, not solely the worker, is viewed as the major cause of*

quality problems: The system is created and can be altered only by the leadership—those who govern or manage the enterprise. They are responsible for ensuring that the system engages in the continuous improvement of its human capital—the men and women who are the employees.

Leadership in the organizations best suited for the new economy is not the same as that in an Era 2, Industrial Age organization. It is no longer the exclusive domain of the president, CEO, or superintendent. In an educational organization, for example, the teacher shares the leadership role with the principal and superintendent in carrying out the dimensions and intentions of quality.

WHAT HAPPENED TO EDUCATION?

Through an historically unparalleled series of events, reports, and forums, stakeholders in the American educational system (students, parents, educators, community members, government, and business) were made aware of, and convinced of, the need to improve elementary and secondary education as a critical means of addressing the grave social, economic, and political problems facing the nation.

Legislatures passed hundreds of statutes aimed at improving education. The existing system was challenged: education, along with business and government, had to be transformed if America was to survive.

At the very time when America needed a highly skilled work force to prevent further losses to commerce, industry, science, and technology, the public education system was not preparing individuals for entry into such a work force. Millions of Americans, some who were high school graduates, were functionally illiterate by even the simplest literacy measures. Business and the military were spending millions of dollars annually to provide remedial education in basic skills for employees and enlistees. Bottom line: the American education system was failing many of its students and the nation.

A BRIEF HISTORY OF CALLS FOR CHANGE
IN EDUCATION

From its beginning, a central aim of all U.S. education is to help the *individual* fulfill his or her capacities to become a thinking person who has learned how to learn. This process was understood to run from immaturity to maturity, from dependence to independence. The development of the self-instructing learner who has learned to organize and guide his or her own learning experiences is not a new goal. In 1873, Herbert Spencer said,

> In education, the process of self-development should be encouraged to the fullest extent. Children should be led to make their own investigations, and to draw their own inferences. They should be *told* as little as possible, and induced to *discover* as much as possible. Humanity has progressed solely by self-instruction; and . . . to achieve best results, each mind must progress somewhat after the same fashion. — *Education: Intellectual, Moral & Physical* (pp. 124–125)

Reformers were making attempts long before computer-assisted and managed learning. In the 1920s, Mary Ward, a supervisor of arithmetic in the San Francisco State Normal School (now San Francisco State University), suggested to her students that they prepare learning materials so that pupils could proceed at their own rate. She found, for example, that the number of days required by each child to complete the "high-second-grade arithmetic" ranged from fewer than 5 to 65 days.

Her university president, Frederic Burke, became excited about her instructional exercises for existing textbooks. Later, many of these exercises were used instead of texts. Individual instruction was widely used in the elementary school attached to the Normal School. A few prominent school systems took up the practice. But the practice could not be sustained; it was overcome by the prevailing (and still continuing) culture of schooling.

President Burke's indictment of the traditional classroom system used in schools: "The class system has been modeled upon the military system. It is constructed upon the assumption that a group of minds can be marshaled and controlled in growth in exactly the same manner that a military officer marshals and directs the bodily movements of a company of soldiers. In solid unbreakable phalanx the class is supposed to move through the grades, keeping in locked step. This locked step is set by the average pupil — an algebraic myth born of inanimate figures and an addled pedagogy."

EDUCATIONAL FADDISM

Since World War II, the history of education is full of examples of proposed changes that are taken up with great enthusiasm for a brief period of time and fail to take root or become part of the mainstream of educational practice.

Typically, these "innovations" involve a small number of interested parties (and are heavily subsidized temporarily by outside funding) and quietly fade away after affecting only a few. Comments from the educator with even a limited experience on the job, such as "this too shall pass" or "here we go again," suggest that many educators have viewed educational change as something to be endured.

This may also help explain why many educators respond to demands for educational change by replying that a major problem in education is the frequency of change. Clearly, in many cases, educational faddism is confused with change.

When change is understood as something distinctly different, it is evident that education has changed very little since its inception in the 1800s. Significant changes in education, when they have occurred, have been responses to legal or societal issues. Desegregation and collective bargaining are just two prime examples.

American educators have relentlessly pursued new programs, texts, and methods in order to improve educational processes but not in engineering their actual widespread use. Observers even note a predictable pattern of shifts every few years so that being familiar with the fleeting nature of educational fads of the past and the predictable shifting of emphases causes some educators to exhibit a nonchalant attitude when recent mandates for change are issued.

WHAT'S DIFFERENT THIS TIME?

During the early 1980s, educators experienced a wave of reform that demanded that teachers and administrators do more of what they had been doing and do it better. The existing educational system was to be fine-tuned by requiring more testing of teachers and students, higher standards for graduation and teacher certification, more closely defined curriculum, more carefully selected textbooks, and more accountability. Coalitions of concerned citizens (parents, educators, elected officials, business and industry leaders, and private citizens) offered solutions to fix education. Fixing education was viewed primarily as a people not a system problem. The existing educational system would improve if people were smarter and worked harder.

By the mid-1980s, it was increasingly clear that these approaches for improvement, prescribed from top-down, were not going to significantly change the situation. Demanding that educators do more of the same or do the same things better did not, and could not, produce the desired results.

To improve, systemic change is an absolute requirement. An out-of-date American educational system, designed in the Agricultural Age and refitted to meet the needs of an industrial age, is ill prepared and cannot meet the needs of an Information Age society.

THE STUDENT AS CUSTOMER

As we have witnessed, quality in the Era 2–3 transition rests on two pillars: fitness for use and customer satisfaction. Satisfaction over time leads to customer loyalty. Loyalty is even more important than satisfaction. Loyalty relates directly to meeting or preferably exceeding the user's expectations.

The Customer/Supplier Model

In this model, suppliers provide inputs that are processed and remade into outputs that are utilized by customers.

- Internal customers (co-workers, employees, teammates) receive the output of internal suppliers; add value through addition, enhancement, or refinement; and in turn become the suppliers back to the internal customers at the next stage of the process. The external customer is the final purchaser or user of the finished product or service.
- Satisfied and loyal customers generate a continuing need for the product and service that allows the organization to stay in business and provide jobs for the members of the organization. Quality is achieved only when everyone in the organization is focused on the same purpose.

- Innovations must contribute to the organization's goal of providing a quality product or service to help the customer lead a better life. Innovations should be introduced only after careful research, the value to the customers is established, the costs are determined, and employees are trained in the use of the innovation.
- Improvement cannot be a one-time effort or project. It may mean incremental improvements to a quality product or creating new products. Improvement is not achieved by focusing solely on results, but by focusing on improving the systems that create the results.

AMERICAN *KAIZEN,* OPHELIMITY, AND EDUCATORS

The development and use of tools and mindsets for identifying and solving problems to further a continuous improvement process is central to ophelimity thinking. Data gathering and data utilization are the important elements.

Many educators soon find that the principles of quality defined herein can be applied to education when adapted and translated for the educational culture and environment.

- Educators understand that *customers* are the people they serve: students, parents, the future employers, and other educators.
- They appreciate the need their customers have for a high-quality education (in the ophelimity sense) that will help them live as productive citizens in a changing world.
- It is not difficult for educators to accept that the customer decides what quality is and not the producer. After all, educators are in the business of making judgments about the quality of work produced by others.

Educators can readily conceptualize education as a *system* made up of many interrelated sub-systems, all of which need to be brought into sharper focus on a common goal. They can see education as an input/output process that takes what is supplied, adds value to it, and then sends it on to the next process. With few exceptions, the concepts associated with producing quality, such as American *kaizen* and ophelimity thinking, apply to education.

The terms *product* and *service* are exceptions, however, and they are important exceptions. The terms *product* and *service* as used in the for-profit industrial age setting – the one the present education mindset is mired in – do not always seem applicable in public education.

- In the business sector, the term *product* generally defines the "something" physical that is produced, e.g., a lamp.
- The term *service* in this environment is most often associated with the attitudes shown while delivering or maintaining the product, such as those of helpful sales clerks or auto repair.
- The quality of the product seems to generate more attention than the quality of the service; for example, a customer might buy a good product even if the service were not outstanding.
- The product is tangible; customer service appears to be an intangible.

Educators do not think of product or service in this way. Educators argue convincingly that

- The product that is produced is learning – a change in human behavior.
- The product – the change in behavior – generally cannot be attributed to a single event or factor.
- The learning experiences (the instructional activities provided) – the service – are more easily documented.
- The service, therefore, appears to be more tangible than the product.

Educators ask: Is quality determined by the product (the changes in the behavior), and, if so, which ones? Or is quality to be determined by judging the learning opportunities (the service), and, if so, which ones? Deciding what to judge or what is important (product or service) is a major source of contemporary confusion and a major obstacle to the needed restructuring.

We know for sure that the Industrial Age distinction between product and service makes no sense in this era of transition to a new knowledge economy. All work is service, because in the new economy everyone in an organization serves customers. Not everyone deals with external customers, but everyone in an organization serves customers, e.g., the person who receives the work of the internal supplier. Quality, then, is determined by the customer's perception of the value received.

> The customer's entire experience determines his (or her) perception of quality. That perception is affected by the organization's "product," processes, and practices as they compare to the customer's expectations. Quality is the measure of the customer's satisfaction with the entire experience.—Albrecht, 1992 (p. 14)

CONSTRUCTING A NEW EDUCATIONAL CULTURE

The Educational Culture

The more things change, the more they stay the same. Drake and Roe (1986) note the various aspects of organization, structure, teaching procedures, and the learning process that prevailed in the 1880s (pp. 176–177) in the United States that are predominant and still applicable to most schools today (Table 7.1).

Table 7.1. Learning Processes in U.S. Schools (circa 1880).

1. Classes are for the most part graded rather than un-graded.
2. Students are taught each subject by a single teacher rather than by a team or series of teachers.
3. Class periods are of a uniform duration, such as 40 to 60 minutes.
4. The school year consists of approximately 180 days.
5. The formal school is held spring, winter, and fall and is closed during the summer months.
6. Academic subjects are given an equal amount of time throughout the school year, no matter what the subject.
7. The academic courses in the school curriculum are essentially the same.
8. The student is expected to complete 4 years of high school before graduation.
9. All classes begin at the beginning of the semester or school year and end at the end of the semester or school year.
10. The formal school day begins at a certain time for students and ends at a certain time for students.
11. Students generally remain in school for 12 to 13 years.
12. An evaluation system, usually letter grading, is provided for pupils that compares them with the group rather than themselves.
13. Most schools have some semblance of a college preparatory, vocational education, and general education track system for students.
14. The school building and the classroom are where formal education takes place.
15. Schools have a superintendent, a principal, and a teacher hierarchy.
16. All schools have a board of education and are part of a state system, and so on.

The sameness found in the way public education is organized and conducted in fifty separate state school systems speaks dramatically to the strength of education's current culture and the role tradition plays in organizations. Schools in the 1990s are not significantly different from those of the 1880s with the exception of size and number.

As a government-directed institution, public education is particularly resistant to change. Public education represents stability in an otherwise chaotic world. With significant changes occurring in the global economy, in religious and other basic institutions, and in human relationships (especially in the family), many people are reluctant to see education change, because it appears to be one of the few anchors in a very stormy sea—one they can romanticize from their own school experience.

"Schools ain't what they used to be and never was."—Will Rogers, American humorist

---

Even when people know that change must occur to meet the needs of society, accepting this need intellectually does not mean that the change is accepted for any real decision making—a function of feeling and emotion.

People are attached to the culture of education by virtue of their common schooling experiences. Changing the culture of education causes people, both educators and the public, to experience loss.

In a very common sense way, culture may be defined as the shared understandings that people in an organization have about how the organization works and about how they work in the organization. Consciously or unconsciously, as people work in an organization they come to internalize how things are done in the organization. They learn about the acceptable standards for behavior, how to treat one another, what the organization really values, and what the rules are for getting the job done. These shared understandings hold the organization together and give it a distinctive identity.

The nature of culture in an organization is portrayed well by Sashkin and Kiser (1993) in their collaborative work with Richard Williams:

> "Culture is the cumulative perception of how the organization treats people and how people expect to treat one another. It is based on *consistent and persistent management action,* as seen by employees, vendors, and customers." (p. 86)

In searching for America's best-run companies, Peters and Waterman (1982) found that culture was closely tied to the success of excellent companies. They noted that the stronger the culture in these companies and the more the culture was directed toward valuing the customer, the fewer policy manuals, organization charts, detailed rules, and procedures were needed. With clearly defined guiding values, people throughout the organization knew what they were supposed to do in almost every situation.

In these companies, there were esteemed heroes and heroines and a strong prevailing mythology. In fact, the culture was so strong in each of these excellent companies that prospective employees made decisions as to whether or not they would explore working for such an enterprise based upon their understanding of its culture and its congruency with their own values and beliefs.

THE GOAL POSTS

If learning was a sport . . .
If subjects in schools were perceived as tools . . .
What do we know for sure when it's game time?

Learning and earning are now inseparable.

- A quality educational system is an absolute essential to the economic, political, and social welfare of the United States.

It's now time to think and work smarter.

- Asking or demanding that people work harder and do more of what has always been done in the way it has always been done will not produce the needed changes or results.

We continue driving down the road with our eyes on the rear-view mirror.

- The current system is structured and organized to meet the needs of an age and society that no longer exist.

The transition is already well underway; the school system must catch up.

- The system must be restructured to meet the needs of a society already in a transition to an enriched cognitive economy and an Information Age.

"This is the way we've always done it around here"—famous last words.

- The concept of restructuring means changing the culture of the enterprise. The culture consists of common understandings about the rules, roles, and relationships between and among employees and stakeholders. It is what one means when one says, "This is what we know that is right about education and how we have always done things."

Business, parents, citizens, and educators must demand better schools.

- Educators cannot make the needed changes in public education alone. Education is government. The "public" nature of the institution makes education the interest and the legitimate partner of all citizens.

Change must be "ground out," yard by yard, as in football.

- The changes needed in education require long-term commitment to improvement. There is no quick fix.

"It's the economy stupid"—slogan of the 1992 Clinton-Gore campaign.

- There is no commonly held general agreement about the purposes and outcomes of public education in America except in one area where there is a growing consensus: The employability skills needed for the new economy.

We need schools to meet the needs of a cognitive-rich, Information Age economy.

- School leaders and policy makers must be committed to the transformation of education to meet more stringent skill and knowledge objectives and to understand what this fully means, or it will not occur.

Leave no stone unturned.

- Every aspect of the educational process and system must be studied and reconsidered in light of new and different societal expectations.

Essential to the success of this endeavor is the development and articulation of the purposes and results of public education at the national, state, and local levels. There must be a shared understanding between educators and their constituents about the goals and outcomes of the joint educational processes.

Facing this challenge boggles the minds of many educators. After more than two decades of almost unrelenting criticism and pressure, many educators are skeptical, disillusioned, and just plain tired. It is understandably threatening to some educators to suggest that they change the system in which they have been successful both as students themselves and as practitioners.

DEMING AND SPORTS: FRAMEWORK FOR IMPROVEMENTS IN EDUCATION

From the perspective of ensuring quality during the ongoing transition from Era 2 (Industrial Age) to Era 3 (Information Age), the Deming TQM (Total Quality Management) principles serve us well in building the playbook:

- *Constancy of purpose:* The total organization is committed to staying in business by meeting or exceeding customer needs, time after time. This requires that everyone in the organization look for continuous improvement of product and services, research and education, and innovation. Constancy of purpose helps everyone work together to move the organization (school or school district) in a single direction with a long-term focus.
- *Continuous improvement:* The total organization is aware of and committed to the ongoing improvement and refinement of products, services, and processes as the means of satisfying the customer. The status quo is not good enough. All processes are

under study at all times. Improvement occurs through both incremental change and through carefully evaluated innovation.

- *Comprehensive perspective:* The organization is viewed as a whole system of inter-connective components. Constancy of purpose is achieved when all the components of a system work toward the same aim: system optimization. Responsibility for the final product or service is shared by all.
- *Customer-driven service:* Quality improvement involves finding out what the customer wants and satisfying the customer again and again. Determining the needs and desires of the customer is an ongoing effort, because customer needs and desires change with time. Systems should be designed to deliver what the customer wants without hassles.
- *School and district culture:* The shared understandings that people in an organization have about how the organization works and about how to work in the organization are its culture. Culture represents the basic mindset, attitudes, and values of the organization.
- *Counting for quality:* Statistical process tools and problem-solving processes are used by everyone in the organization to analyze, understand, and solve quality improvement problems. The use of the most important tools — brainpower and rational thinking — needs to be encouraged. Decisions are made on the basis of data and not opinions, assumptions, and habits.
- *Decentralized decision making:* Within the framework of the total system, decision making for quality improvement purposes is decentralized to empower those closest to the point of improvement. An integral part of decentralization is internal communication. Roles, responsibilities, and relationships are affected by decentralization.
- *Collegial leadership:* Barriers between people and departments are eliminated. Teamwork and cooperation are encouraged so that employees can concentrate on the purpose of quality improvement. "Quality is job one," says the Ford commercial. Knowledge, resources, ideas, and solutions are pooled in order to solve problems.

CHAPTER 8

Solutions—Work Force Development and Winning

> "Football success is desire and speed and intelligence—and desire is 85 percent of it."—Retired Coach "Bud" Wilkinson, University of Oklahoma

THERE ARE MANY legendary stories about Coach George Allen. In 1966, Allen took over the head coaching job of the Los Angeles Rams. Roman Gabriel, who quarterbacked the Rams for 11 years and was voted NFL's Most Valuable Player in 1969 says this of Allen, "His whole life was devoted to winning football games. He never had a driver's license or car because he claimed he couldn't think about football when he was driving. He always used a driver who picked him up and drove him to practice or to do errands. George needed to think about football at all times."

George Allen, then also the Rams' general manager, would meet personally with players to talk contracts. But, sooner or later, the talks turned to football strategy and tactics—to solutions for winning. "Once, during contract negotiations, George and I met at a local golf course for lunch," said Gabriel. "George wasn't as good a negotiator as he was a coach. He always seemed to get sidetracked away from negotiation.

"I remember we both ordered roast beef, mashed potatoes and peas during negotiation. As we were eating, he was talking about certain defenses he wanted to use during the upcoming season and he would get more and more excited. Pretty soon he had cut up his roast beef into small pieces and was using the beef to diagram plays on his plate. Of course, he was a defensive-oriented coach and he used the roast beef as his defensive players. The peas were soft and mushy so they were the offensive players. The contract never got discussed."

At this point in our book, it is tempting to offer up a long series of checklists and tables to guide readers in building their own playbook. How do you build ophelimity thinking—customer-centered quality—into a working model? We know what works—it's praxis makes perfect. Which are the best plays of the playbook and in what order should we run the plays? Who should take the lead in setting up American *kaizen*—continuous improvement linking breakthrough and control? Which technologies should be called upon to bring about American *kaizen?* How do we break the zero-sum mindset and employ coopetition (teamwork and competition) to achieve a winning formula? Some of these questions have been illustrated and answered in part throughout this book. But trying to specifically answer all these questions at this point would be a mistake.

Part of the answer lies in what Dallas Cowboys' Coach Barry Switzer said, "There is no magic playbook. There's no magic way to do things. There's so many different ways to do things. If there weren't, all the teams would have the same plays in their playbook." The underlying principles are the same; the execution is different.

Internet addresses signal the new language of a world embedded in technology. Only a few years back, the cable company and the phone company were looked upon as totally different service businesses. Today, depending on with whom you talk and what the latest news is coming across the evening business news or *The Wall Street Journal,* each is entering the other's business or more properly fusing the technologies. The impact has already been felt and is sure to have significant effects on students, teachers, businesses, and our way of life.

An analog with which to view the impact of exponentially larger capacities to move information can be helpful. Standing on the side of the road of the so-called Information Superhighway, it is hard to visualize what is taking place. The remarkable jumps in bandwidth capacities for a fused cable-phone system to transmit or receive information across the surface of the globe in the blink of an eye is evolving so quickly as to sometimes not even catch our attention. Using glass fiber the size of a human hair can deliver each issue of *The Wall Street Journal* in less than a second. Consider Table 8.1 as a benchmark of the new speed of information.

It takes little imagination to see that still more changes are coming

Table 8.1.

Category	Bandwidth	Bits/Second	Analogy
Telephone Service		64,000	walking path
ISDN Line	2 X Phone Service	128,000	city sidewalk
T1 Line	12 X ISDN	1,544,000	4-lane roadway
T2 Line	28 X T1	43,232,000	112-lane expressway

that will surely place increasingly greater demands on Information Age workers and their need for lifelong learning. Today, schools and business need to open the bandwidth between teachers and students, managers and workers—between coaches and players.

High-speed user access is increasing geometrically, also. Consider the acceleration in download time for a 16 MB image, in minutes (Kbps = Kilobytes per second):

- using a 14.4 Kbps phone modem: 16.52 minutes
- using a 28.8 Kbps phone modem: 9.26 minutes
- using a 128 Kbps ISDN phone high-speed modem: 2.08 minutes
- using a 10 Mbps cable modem: 0.03 minutes

GETTING OUR ARMS AROUND LARGE PROBLEMS— ANOTHER ELEPHANT

> Ophelimity means challenging conventional views of training, teaching, and learning.

Doing business halfway around the world is qualitatively different from doing it in Kansas City. You operate within a different business climate. You are producing products or delivering goods and services to people with a totally different culture than our own. Make no mistake about it: if you are doing business in Kansas City today, you are competing in a global economy. In a global economy, "my company" can service downtown Kansas City from anywhere in the world just as easily as can "your local company." It's time to revive the old Broadway show tune with a new twist—"It's time to bring everything up-to-date in Kansas City."

Sometimes we are just slow learners. For many years, we romanti-
cized the idea of Americanizing global tastes and styles—rock music,
Big Macs, T-shirts, blue jeans. Yet, it took U.S. auto makers over 40
years to build a right-side steering car for the Japan home market.
As in England, the Japanese drive on the wrong side of the road.
How long would it have taken Toyota, Nissan, and Honda collectively
to capture one-third of the U.S. auto market had they not put the steering wheel on the left side?

Let's take a quick look at U.S. regional markets for an everyday product—coffee—to illustrate once again the principles of ophelimity. Taste
preferences come from cultural and settlement patterns.

- An everyday cup of coffee in Houma, Louisiana, is a thick,
  chicory-based product, more like after-dinner espresso served in
  a New York restaurant.
- Cappuccino bars dot the Seattle landscape, resulting in that city
  having been dubbed the caffeine capital of the U.S.
- Decaffeinated coffee is the big seller in Florida, where over 25
  percent of the state's residents are seniors.

If U.S. regional variations in coffee present such subtle variations,
imagine what awaits our fledgling high school and college graduates
entering the "cyber-café" of the global economy!

MOLDING TODAY'S PLAYER FOR TOMORROW'S GAME

It bears repeating. On the field, the experienced coach takes the time
and maintains patience to bring along young athletes, both in physical
skills and mental dexterity. After every play, players look to their coach
for feedback: response, approval, body language. If the player is
denied this component, he will soon become doubtful, disgruntled,
and ineffectual. But it is especially gratifying when an athlete (or student or worker) appreciates the coach (or a teacher or manager) and
considers him or her a friend in the bigger game of life. This, too, is
a powerful part of coaching (or teaching or managing).

In sports, as in education and business, the successful coach is an active listener as well. The coach (or teacher or manager) can never
assume the athlete (or student or worker) has been sufficiently motivated. Providing continuous feedback becomes increasingly necessary

to both determine what incentives the person is looking for and before a coach can pass judgment on an individual player. Finally, a good coach lets his athletes (or students or workers) know he's always accessible for a one-on-one talk in private. These are the essentials of good coaching practices.

ADD EMPOWERMENT—CUSTOMER AND CO-WORKER SATISFACTION

A remarkable attribute of human beings is our capacity to deliberately, as an act of will, shift how we view what is real. As an act of personal volition, I can choose to see the same thing in different ways and different things in the same ways.

The power to command how we choose to see the world of people, places, and things—and thus, how we shall think about them and then act toward them—holds awesome potential for improving our roles and rules in education and training.

Our perceptions of what is real are governed by the frames or lenses or mental models through which we view what is real. We come into the world equipped to sense it. We have both the anatomy and the physiology to see, hear, smell, taste, and feel it in all its magnitude, complexity, and charm. But we are not prepared to make sense of it. We have to learn how to make sense of it. We have to learn how to *perceive* our world.

We make sense of the world by means of mental models (paradigms) learned through our education and training from birth onward. Ophelimity thinking requires a paradigm shift. Caring is its cornerstone. It is the required shift to power the end result: fitness for use as judged by the user.

When a teacher, coach, or manager uses ophelimity—"fitness for use as judged by the user"—as an action solution, he or she uses seven steps:

- First, they talk and think about a whole new way of seeing things.
- Second, they use intrinsic motivation to power improvement.
- Third, they know that to avoid thinking is more convenient but dangerous.

- Fourth, they recognize each individual's skills, talents, and abilities.
- Fifth, they instruct by explaining *why* from the user's point-of-view.
- Sixth, they take personal charge of continuous improvement.
- Last, they begin with the end in mind — a strong, guiding, and inspiring purpose.

"You've got to have a clear-cut philosophy to be successful, and it must be transmitted to your players. They must thoroughly understand everything you are trying to do, so much so that it eventually simply becomes instinctive to them. . . . We want to be on the same path and know where we are going and what our goals are."—Tom Landry, Coach of the Dallas Cowboys for 27 years.

NOW, ADD MOTIVATION TO THE GOALS

Ever notice when driving through a highway construction area that there are an abundance of warning signs? The standard orange "Men at Work" sign, posted along with flags and cones, seems to be an overstatement. George Allen has suggested some changes:

- "Men Talking"
- "Men Sitting"
- "Men Standing"
- "Men Listening"

Ever notice that sometimes one guy seems to be out there doing the "pick-and-shovel" work while the others are leaning on their shovels, drinking coffee, taking a smoke, or just putting in their time? The crew needs motivation. Only one man is carrying the load.

ADD PERSISTENCE TO KEEP MOVING TOWARD THE GOAL LINE

Continuous improvement requires *rational thinking* to test hypotheses about improved teaching and learning and *creative thinking* to initially stimulate a hypotheses.

Persistence is important in fusing these, because change is never easy for the coach/teacher or the player/student. There are undoubtedly failures, and usually at the most difficult time: at the beginning of the efforts.

In virtually every sport, Karl Mecklenburg was the last guy chosen for the team. In high school, he was cut from the basketball, baseball, and hockey teams. As a last resort, he decided to try football. He's been trying to prove himself since.

By the time he was a senior, he became a prep football star. But not one college offered him a football scholarship. His only choice left was to enroll at the University of Minnesota and try his luck as a walk-on player. He eventually became a starter.

When the NFL draft rolled around his senior year, scouts said he had no chance to make it as a pro, the same story he had heard in high school and college. But the Denver Broncos gambled and picked Mecklenburg in the final round of the 1983 draft. Now all he needed was a fair chance. He made the team still feeling he had something to prove.

His chance came early against the Los Angeles (now Oakland) Raiders. It was Raiders running back Marcus Allen, whose reputation for avoiding a direct hit, became the scapegoat for Mecklenburg's years of "getting no respect."

In the second quarter, with the Raiders leading Denver 7-6, Marcus Allen was about to take a pass in the left flat. The ball had barely reached the Raiders' star when Mecklenburg exploded, running over him, hitting Allen shoulder high with full force. Allen's head snapped back, and he landed with a crunch as the pass fell incomplete.

When the Broncos' defensive coach saw the damage Mecklenburg created, he developed playbook defensive schemes especially suited for his new linebacker. In 1985, against the Pittsburgh Steelers, Mecklenberg played all four linebacker positions and all three positions as a down lineman. In that year, he also recorded a Bronco team record: thirteen quarterback sacks.

What other reason could there be for the failure of most reform efforts at all levels of our educational system, but that they are difficult and risky. Easier, safer methods are always available: easier because they don't require as much time or effort, and safer because they are less likely to reveal mistakes, problems, and failures.

ADD TECHNOLOGY—USING SMART TOOLS

Technology is another player on the team now. Each NFL team uses wireless communications, game films, computer simulations, and sophisticated timing devices to sharpen the skills of each player. Each NASA space shot demonstrates the man-machine relationship and smart team. Mission success and astronaut survival depends on it. Today, repairing a late-model car means bypassing ATM-controlled, self-service, gas pumps to reach a service center capable of electronically analyzing problems and taking corrective action. With the tools of technology and continuous learning, the Era 2 grease monkey has evolved into an Era 3 higher-order cognitive technician capable of reprogramming or replacing a chip-set controlling your car. Trial and error is replaced by diagnosis.

The development of Intranet services (intended to serve the organization and its extended members) reflects the movement to decentralize operations for improved customer service. TSS, an IBM division, contracts with sellers of personal computers to provide hardware and software repair services to the end-user. Mail-order houses Gateway 2000 and Dell and computer superstore CompUSA contract with TSS for on-site computer service. Technicians work independently—kept informed of scheduling and service updates by daily e-mail taken from their laptop computer. They remain on-call through pagers. Technicians at Amdahl Computer use tools to access from any location directly into a customer's mainframe computer with a linked laptop. Corrective action is taken from the remote location. These are the new knowledge workers who operate independently with full management support provided by electronic communications.

We have always depended on tools.

- The Stone Age, the Bronze Age, and the Iron Age were marked by tools made with materials and artifacts produced by those tools.
- The Agricultural Age was possible because of human and animal power and tools that grew up around their use.
- The Industrial Age harnessed energy created by water, steam, and oil into electricity—tools of that era.

The Information Age brings with it cognitive (thinking) tools. As did the cave man before us, we are able to use what works, without necessarily knowing why it works.

FACILITATING CHANGE

Let's face it. We may talk a lot about change, but who really wants to change? I may say I'll change, but what I really mean is, "I'll enjoy watching you change." It's no accident that economics, the dismal science, stresses change. Change is the dismal part of the dismal science.

Change impacts almost every aspect of our lives: political, social, and psychological. It is how our economic lives are jolted. This new, global economy we speak of is born of awesome change. It is at the same time both full of promise and a dire immediate threat.

Awesome change is both frustrating and exhilarating. It jars our mental pictures of what is right and wrong; it attacks our mindset of what is valuable and what must be given up. In our time, change, in both its nature and acceleration, is a form of cognitive warfare; it is an assault upon the lenses through which we make sense of the world.

Paradigm change is transformation that fuses new and old ideas into a powerful synthesis—a new perspective—the insight that allows information to come together in a new form. Another synonym is mental model, the "picture" we carry in the mind. "The good old days" is a mental model. Thus, paradigm change can heal the delusion of either-or; this-or-that. Both players and coaches now practice change. Consider this:

- Today there is almost always more than one right answer.
- Paradigms too strongly held lead to a terminal disease of certainty.
- Paradigm flexibility is the best approach in a world of turmoil and change.
- Paradigms, based on the short-run results, prove counterintuitive long-term.

To grasp the significance of global economic change, it bears remembering that paradigms are a mindset, deeply ingrained assumptions or generalizations that influence and determine how we see the world and how and why we take the actions that we take. Keep in mind that we can choose to change our view of the world.

FORESTALLING TOO MUCH CHANGE

How much change to attempt has important consequences. But, two conflicting principles can help us persist. First, don't try to make too many changes at once. You might not need to change the whole system at once.

This principle has both a scientific and a practical basis. Introducing too many new variables at the same time makes it difficult to separate their effects. While a strictly controlled experiment is not the goal, it's much easier to understand a system with a few modified variables than many. Making gradual, incremental changes is easier and less frightening than a sudden and complete overhaul in course. You'll be more likely to keep doing those things that work and less likely to be overwhelmed and throw the whole thing out, the successes as well as the failures.

Second, small changes may fail when they come into conflict with other aspects of the learning environment.

- Sometimes student expectations or the entrenched functioning of our institutions or even the classroom atmosphere, after years of habit, create barriers to change.
- Sometimes there isn't anything that can be done about these barriers, but just recognizing them is a start and can help.
- Sometimes there are things that can be done to eliminate or alleviate them.
- Sometimes just being patient, and starting over with the next class, is best.

While recognizing that there may actually be something wrong with what you're trying to do, don't immediately assume that it didn't work because it failed once before. Give it another shot, and consider the possible barriers and how to get around them.

LEARNING AND EARNING

Fact is a great dictator! It is possible to ignore, deny, or wish away a fact if the consequences of the ignoring are not immediate, or dramatic, or particularly noticeable. Millions of people prove that fact by ignoring the health warnings on the cigarette packs they buy and then light up. The consequences, though statistically factual of course, occur at a much later date.

There are some facts that cannot be ignored, or denied, or wished away. They demand immediate attention. A toothache, a flat tire, and a bounced check are prime examples. The effects of America's changing economy are, for many Americans, facts that demand immediate attention. They are the ones who have been downsized and lost buying power and former health, pension, and other employment benefits. All Americans are at least becoming aware of the economic facts of life, and there is a growing sense of urgency that something be done about them. Twenty-five percent of U.S. workers reported in a 1996 pre-election poll that they were worried about losing their present job.

There is an unmistakable tie that binds education and the economy together. It is clearer now. Having explored the facts about the new economy as they affect what we teach, to whom, when it is learned, and how that teaching is done, we have learned the central fact we face as a nation. The ways we must earn our living and the requirements to earn a decent living are changing even as we write and you read these words. We now know it has brought about the situation where education as traditionally delivered in our schools and colleges is more and more unconnected to what graduates need to know and how they need to perform to survive and flourish in the economy.

Like people of 18th century Great Britain, Americans now live in a transition period between two economic eras. For the English, it was the transition between the Agricultural and the Industrial Age; for us, it is the transition between the Industrial Age to one not yet officially named, but already bearing such vivid descriptors as *Knowledge and Information Era, Post-Industrial Era, Digital Era,* and *Information Age.*

What we know for sure is that we are riding out the waves of the transition, right now, and with great speed and with personal stress to many; because to them, in the words of the angel in *Green Pastures,* "everything nailed down seems to be coming loose!" Here, to name just a few, are some of the stressors:

- Yesterday, natural resources defined economic power. Today, knowledge is power.

- Yesterday, hierarchy was the model for organizational management structure. Today, it is more horizontal and participative.
- Yesterday, leaders used command and control. Today, leaders empower, mentor, teach, and coach.
- Yesterday, leaders were more like warriors in military environments. Today, leaders are facilitators for others to flourish.
- Yesterday, leaders *demanded* respect. Today, leaders try to *earn* respect.
- Yesterday, producers of products and services defined quality. Today, customers determine fitness for use.
- Yesterday, employees took orders. Today, teams make decisions.
- Yesterday, managers directed, and supervisors flourished. Today, managers delegate, and supervisors vanish.
- Yesterday, everyone was a competitor. Today, competitors also practice collaboration.
- Yesterday, quality was thought to be "nice" to achieve. Today, quality can literally determine survival in the marketplace.

More changes are crammed into each day of our lives than our grandparents experienced in decades, and change driven by new information technologies is still in its earliest stages. It has been said that today our lives are like dog years—each year is equal to 7. Consider for a moment that a musical birthday card today has more computing power than existed on the planet before 1950.

Studying the impact of technology on society over the past 250 years, scholars have developed a surprisingly accurate model for predicting how an economy and a society will interact under these impacts.

The Impact of Technology on Society
- New knowledge leads to new technology.
- The new technology causes economic changes.
- The economic changes, in turn, cause social and political change.
- The result—creation of new paradigms—a new reality and what should be done.

BUILDING HUMAN CAPITAL FOR THE EMERGING ERA

In the new era, whatever it ends up being called officially, one thing is certain. Those who'll earn the best living for themselves and their families and have the best quality of life will be those who cultivate and actualize human capital. Those who merely exhibit underdeveloped human capital—the unskilled and undereducated—will be relegated to compete globally with those earning the least desirable living. The real danger is in not understanding that if a community, or a state, or the U.S. wishes to attract and sustain high-wage, economically sound jobs, *all* its people must learn to think and work smarter.

If you follow the newspapers, read professional or business magazines, or take in TV specials on the economy, you are aware of the massive transformations taking place. But, despite increasing awareness, few fully grasp its implications for their own well-being as well as for American society in general. Fewer still have recognized the economic and social implications of a new era built on enriched cognitive labor. Even fewer yet are aware of its implications for the schools and colleges and for learning in general.

Like a secured and marked path to safety through a jungle wrought with minefields through hostile territory, America's only secure and marked path to economic success now runs through its schools and colleges. Formal education—tuned to an information-rich, global economy—now stands as the gateway to individual economic ability. The correlation between the number of years attended, the degrees and certificates awarded, and the amount of money a person earns has repeatedly been demonstrated to be an almost perfect fit.

While there are always exceptions to the general rule, it is foolhardy at a minimum, and dangerous at best, to assume one will become an exception: a high-tech billionaire Bill Gates or a multi-millionaire pro football player Deion Sanders. Penn State University football Coach Joe Paterno captured it well in a public service TV announcement: "Only one in 10,000 kids playing high school football will make it to the pros. Don't make a mistake. Stay in school and get an education."

Educators now find themselves at the top of the nation's priorities for increased scrutiny and improvement. How has this direct relationship between jobs and education and the creation and maintenance of higher paying jobs that depend on better educated workers come about? What are the implications and consequences of education now being seen as the nation's most important business? And most importantly, how can this institution change to meet its new obligations? These are the seminal questions that have been addressed by us.

The reader will have found in this book no blaming, no scape-goating, no excuses. What has been presented are guides to a playbook for successfully meeting the challenges of the "big game." It has bridged ideas to implementation. Now, it's your turn for action.

According to the 1994 World Competitiveness Report:

- Taiwan ranked the best in the world with 94 percent overall literacy and an extensive system of higher education.
- Singapore's male literacy rate was 95 percent and 83 percent for females—ranked at the top for an education system structured to meet the needs of a competitive economy.
- Israel's adult literacy is 95 percent; 27 percent of the population have attended college. In 1993, 70 percent of all immigrants moving to Israel were experienced in techno-scientific fields.
- In 1970, Poland's illiteracy rate for its entire population was 2.2 percent; its colleges have introduced the "techno-MBA," combining business and technical education.

Our nation must also develop a more integrated work force. By the turn of the century, a growing percentage of our public school students will be Black or Hispanic. Simple justice continues to demand that each student be allowed and encouraged to fulfill her or his potential, regardless of race or ethnic background. The demand for a more competitive human capital now makes the need for carrying out this simple justice a necessity for economic survival. We cannot successfully survive with a multi-polar nation.

If you are a coach fielding a team to win its share of games in an intensely competitive multi-cultural global economy, what more valuable human asset could you want on your side than a skilled and trained, ethnically diverse mix of workers? Only America has the potential to educate, train and field a team with those characteristics.

One of the major factors leading to coopetition being built into the new playbook is to bring participants into the process of cooperation with competitors.

First, they see themselves working side by side, not as adversaries. Today, we team; tomorrow, we compete as the Silicon Glen example demonstrates. Next, the focus turns to identifying and concentrating on mutual interests, not specific circumstances. There are lots of battles to win on the global playing field, and there are many different theaters of operation. Just watch computers and bio-medicine. They considered plenty of options for building mutual interests: design, production, marketing, support services, to name a few. Then, all parties seek fair and impartial measurements for building mutual trust among the participants. The end game is spelled out up front so the players and coaches down on the field can read the scoreboard results together.

Three challenges – (1) the demand for more knowledge and skills, (2) new knowledge and skills, and (3) more broadly shared and distributed knowledge and skills – stand out as the requirements for improving (1) what we teach, (2) when it is taught, (3) to whom it is taught, and (4) how it is taught.

Schools, as a basic economic necessity for the nation, will look for ways to teach more efficiently and effectively, to teach new things as well as what has been found to be basic, and to reach student populations long neglected or underserved. We know that schools, like other aspects of government, rarely embrace real change without difficulty.

We are reminded of a story of a man running for political office. He had just returned from seeing one of the world's great volcanoes erupt. He describes in stark detail the power, majesty, and force that the fire and spewing lava had wrought on everything in its path. He likened this event to the changes facing us from the new global economy – the crashing together of Thurow's global tectonic plates. His opponent, in cynical political style, dismisses these warnings with the boast that "We have a volunteer fire department back home that could put that thing out in 15 minutes." This time, we fear the warning is justified and the dismissal foolhardy.

There are certain built-in obstacles to change that can be identified and successfully overcome. Here is just one well-known example. Tax dollars now come to schools regardless of their learning effectiveness. The school's "customers" have little or even no choice but to send their students to their assigned school. Of course, they pay for a private school if they have the funds or move their place of residence, which many have done.

WE KNOW A GREAT DEAL ABOUT HOW PEOPLE LEARN EFFECTIVELY

We also know a great deal *more* than previously about how people learn effectively. We know the best conditions under which people can apply their knowledge to new situations. Research-based knowledge challenges what still goes on today in our schools and colleges. It disclaims a traditional school model.

The optimal characteristics of the new effective learning experience needs to

- be organized to deliver learning efficiently
- reflect workplace knowledge demands and work contexts in which knowledge and skills have to be used
- develop knowledge and skills that are broadly applicable
- blur the division between academic and vocational learning

It builds upon (1) what people need to know and the know-how to do in nonschool settings, and (2) how people learn most naturally and effectively.

Corporate investment in human capital remains key to advancing a new model of corporate citizenship. It is based on treating workers as balance sheet assets—assets to be developed and improved upon rather than costs to be cut. To value a worker means investing in his or her training, not just in college graduates who receive the bulk of the $40 billion that companies spend each year on training, but the frontline workers who are at the heart of any organization.

It would be preposterous to think of a football team limiting special coaching to just the backfield—the quarterback and running backs. A football team commits coaching resources for every position—the center, guards, tackles, ends, linebackers, safety, kickers, defense specialists, and on and on. In football, it is self-evident that each player and the entire team must perform up to competitive standards. So, too, the same within any organization. The best companies now reportedly devote at least 1.5 to 2 percent of their payrolls to upgrading the skills of their own workers.

> "It is no news to business leaders that a skilled work force can be a strategic trump card. Other elements of a business—machines, processes, raw materials, access to finance and cheap labor—can be replicated by competitors. But a skilled, flexible, involved work force can create value in ways that matter in the marketplace and offer an enduring competitive advantage."—Robert Reich, former Clinton Administration Secretary of Labor

A LEARNING COMMONWEALTH: SCHOOLS, PARENTS, COMMUNITY, BUSINESS PARTNERSHIP

Students learn as much in the community, from the media, and in their homes as they do in schools. Students need increased opportunities to utilize their learning in the community through internships, community service, establishing student enterprises, and through participating in community-based learning. Similarly, community members need to be in the schools to support and extend student work and learning. Schools cannot do it alone. As the African proverb says (and Hillary Clinton's book is titled), "It takes a village to raise a child."

Learning communities work collaboratively to make this a reality, not rhetoric. Partnership is not about "buy-in"; it is about authentic involvement, participation, shared leadership, and shared decision making. Involving key people from "outside" the school is essential to establishing the school as part of a collaborative learning community. None of this is possible without the involvement—right from the start and continuously throughout the change process—of parents and community people.

To create a learning commonwealth, one needs to operate systemically:

- To think whole rather than parts. It is the story of the blind man and the elephant.
- To think relationships rather than individuals or separated objects. It is team play.
- To think process rather than structure. It is a playbook rather than a game plan.
- To think networks rather than hierarchy. It is teamwork.
- To think quality rather than quantity. It is ophelimity, fitness for use judged by users.
- To think sufficiency rather than scarcity. It is thinking and working smarter.
- To think dynamic balance rather than constant growth. It is control and breakthrough.
- To think interdependence rather than autonomy. It is winning teams, not star power.
- To think cooperation rather than competition. It is coopetition as resource conservation.

- To think approximation rather than absolute truth. It is recognizing patterns of change.
- To think partnership rather than domination. It is win-win.

The foundation of a learning commonwealth is collaboration—working together for common goals, partnership, shared leadership, co-evolving, and co-learning—rather than competition and power given to only a few.

Gene Maeroff, President of the *New York Times* Education Foundation and Dean of Education Journalists, put it right on the line, "In schools, disciplines are as separate as the planets." Thus far, it has been difficult for educators to even imagine the far-reaching possibilities of collaboration.

The focus of the learning commonwealth is students actively demonstrating their understanding, rather than students passing written tests as the sole sign of knowing. Learning is based on conceptual understanding and the ability to apply knowledge in a variety of contexts. Putting the focus on student learning, rather than the teacher "covering the content" also means

- students taking more responsibility for their own learning
- learning experiences geared to students' interests and needs
- students actively engaged in learning in a variety of groups and contexts
- learning as applied, internalized, and understood

Collaboration and learning happen within the context of community—a unity that celebrates diversity. Communities are not the arithmetic total of its individuals but the interaction among individuals themselves. It means "concentrating on what happens between the buildings, not the buildings themselves," said community-builder Jim Rouse.

The school reflects the population and background of the larger community. A learning commonwealth helps students learn the attitudes, knowledge, and skills that benefit all in their community. It allows, no demands, community members to become partners in facilitating and expanding the learning process.

During this transformation, "no one knows who will be a dinosaur and who will be a mammal," writes MIT's Thurow. "That depends upon who is the best at adjusting to a new world—something that can only be known with certainty looking backward."

We have examined what we think education is, what we see as desired outcomes for students, and how we think learning should become more focused in the face of the global economic challenge to our way of life. We have talked about the need to distinguish the powerful factors rooted in what is, no doubt, this nation's greatest challenge since its founding and the winning of World War II – to bring the performance of its students, workers, and citizenry up to world-class competitive performance standards.

Action and solutions come about from more than following a checklist of factors. They are as much a mindset as a map. A renewed accountability for the craft of teaching, personal development, and the caring for our students, workers, and customers will help ensure America's economic future. It is now the preface to building your own playbook.

CHAPTER 9

Guidelines for Building the Playbook for Education

WHEN LEON LESSINGER was Dean of the College of Education at the University of South Carolina a faculty member related a story about a man who was given an original of a cartoon as a gift. It had been drawn by B. Tobey and published in the *New Yorker Magazine*.

The cartoon depicts a middle-aged man in his robe and pajamas. He stands in front of his house gazing thoughtfully at the night sky. From an upstairs window his wife calls to him anxiously. "All right," she says, "but promise you'll come in and go to bed the instant you *do* discover the meaning of it all."

We can't guarantee that the football metaphor translated into a practical *educator's playbook* will supply that need. But we can assure the reader that it will go a long way toward helping produce observable benefits and even uncover interesting new directions for progress in education.

THE PLAYBOOK—PUTTING SOLUTION TALK INTO ACTION

Newspapers, magazines, books, the media, and talk shows, to name but a few, are full of problem talk about education—even of hand-wringing. There are tens of thousands of pages lining bookstore shelves that bemoan our schools. But *Game Time: The Educator's Playbook for the New Global Economy* focuses on solutions.

Your playbook can be a repository of "solution talk" and stand in marked contrast to the omnipresent "problem talk." A simple charting of the many conversations among school faculty shows clearly the extent of problem versus solution talk. In fact, such charting has been done. And the result? As much as 90% of the time, conversations among educators on the job focus on problems and not on solutions.

There are several reasons for this phenomenon. Sometimes problems persist simply by the fact that people think and talk about them incessantly. Further, the past is mostly seen as a source of problems; few have been trained to see them equally clearly as a potential resource for solutions.

A colleague wrote three books while recovering from prostate cancer treatment. He described this achievement as having spent his time "squeezing lemons into lemonade."

There is a marked tendency to use psychiatric, sociological, and psychological terminology when describing unresolved problems. These terms can be replaced by different, and even more accurate, terminology. Probably the most powerful way to shift from "unresolved problem talk" to "solution towards results" talk is to understand, practice and use different paradigms. A well crafted playbook can supply one of these paradigms and help deal with many of the other major reasons.

Shortly we will erect a "scaffold" whose rungs contain major elements of the football metaphor, all of which have particular relevance for improving teaching and learning in schools and colleges.

After understanding, comes action. We know what has to be done. The building of your playbook is the most important step to take. What follows are a set of guidelines flowing from the football metaphor and upon which you can now hang your own ideas for school improvement.

THE FOOTBALL METAPHOR SCAFFOLD OF IDEAS

(*1*) New Beginnings and Adjustment to Change

(*2*) The Importance of Human Capital

(*3*) The Attractiveness of Diversity

(*4*) Service to Customers: Ophelimity Thinking

(*5*) Continuous Improvement, Breakthrough, Control, and a Discipline of Caring

(*6*) Continuous Use and Upgrading of Technology

(*7*) Coaching and Leadership of Specialists

(*8*) Coopetition: Simultaneous Collaboration and Competition

(*9*) Praxis "Makes Perfect"

(*10*) Practice "Makes Perfect"

NEW BEGINNINGS AND ADJUSTMENT TO CHANGE

Every game and every season is different. Football demonstrates continuous adjustment to change. Each new season is a new beginning. It's a chance to put a losing season behind us and to wipe the slate clean. And, last year's winners cannot rest on their laurels. Losers are not preordained to repeat mistakes. Winners may not always continue winning. Both winners and losers face new challenges on a fast, ever-changing, playing field.

Each team does its homework. The more resolute usually do better. Those who scout the other teams – both new talent and new coaches – ready themselves for the battle. These players are better prepared to dominate the game as well as adapt to lots of game day surprises.

Television has generated thousands of fans who regularly watch NFL football. The big plays, on-the-field antics, the color and pageantry of the game add to the viewer's experience.

Whenever it's *Game Time* the NFL match-up is three things – sports, entertainment, and big business. Hidden from view is the enormous variety of factors at work among players on the field – especially a consistently winning team.

It takes the mastery of many subtleties to mold world-class players – for them to learn how to quickly and positively adapt to a constantly changing contest. The winning player has an automated knowledge of fundamentals combined with superior physical and mental conditioning.

Through professional sports we are able to recognize the impact of gradual and rapid change as it affects the system. The game that emerges as the minutes click off the clock results from subtle changes. Deep and turbulent events cause the playbook to be altered which, in turn, governs the playing of the game and which also changes the game forever.

The evolution of U.S. sports has been marked by unorthodox and convulsive change events. Though now quite familiar to players and fans, these turning points helped forge kinds of players, coaches, game plans, and the playbook in use today.

THE IMPORTANCE OF HUMAN CAPITAL

Every coach and fan understands that the game of professional football was and is built and made popular by the players. Owners, coaches, fans, economic stakeholders, owe them everything.

The success of a play, a game, or a season often comes down to the individual effort of one player. Fans can see this easily by focusing on the quarterback, whose mistakes cost touchdowns, or on the kicker to name only two positions.

Every player of team sports knows his team cannot defeat its opponent without each player's mastery of the essentials. Precision thinking, strategy, and physical prowess are indispensable parts of the "machine." Every player knows that the actions called for in the playbook are for naught if any teammate fails in their individual tasks. Players are drilled with the knowledge that you have to make the play when the ball is there. You've got to make it now!

Human capital is the economist's term to describe skilled, educated people. The concept of human capital was known to economists as early as the eighteenth century. Serious work on the economic theory of human capital, however, is relatively new. The term itself first appeared in an article in the *American Economic Review* (1961) entitled "Investment in Human Capital" by Nobel Prize-winning economist Theodore W. Schultz.

To some it may seem foreign that knowledge can be considered a form of capital. The dictionary defines *capital* as "any form of wealth employed for the production of more wealth." Because of our immersion in the mindset of the Industrial Age, it is common to think of a machine, like an auto assembly line, as capital equipment if it produces wealth. But physicians' skill and education produce wealth for them in the form of considerably higher than average income, so medical knowledge and skill can be legitimately considered to be capital as well. Acquiring a medical education is a major kind of capital investment—a doctor can be viewed as "capital knowledge" in human form, or *human capital*. A similar statement can be made about anyone who has learned what he or she needs to know or be able to do to satisfy "customers." In the NFL human capital is summed up in the three S's — speed, strength, and smarts.

THE ATTRACTIVENESS OF DIVERSITY

Save for talent, there is no discrimination in playing for the NFL. The explosion of interest in professional football among the fans and the sheer devotion to the game crosses ethnic, racial, social, economic, and intellectual lines. Executives are season ticket holders along with their employees. A good percentage of any pro football crowd is made up of women. The kids flock by the thousands.

Players come from across the nation. They are brash, bashful, quiet, loud, tall, short. All of them are strong and quick and very skillful at their trade. Their chance of making it is small indeed, since at best only three or four of the thirty-odd rookies in a pro training camp will stick with the team.

Some of them are college All-Americans, fresh from stardom. Others played on small-college teams, and the big city is a new experience. The rookies are nervous and subdued while the old pros chat easily about the season coming and the season past.

Today's players are different. Until the late 1960s, athletes were developed in a very regimented and highly disciplined manner. The crew haircut (short flat-top military style) was in. Training habits, sleep, no smoking, no booze helped concentrate the player's mind on health and fitness for the game. Coaching staffs were given a high degree of respect, routinely called mister, and rapid motivation was the norm. Coaches worked within a pretty well accepted set of guidelines, and players knew and accepted exactly what was expected of them at all times.

"Bad boy" Joe Namath changed all that as well as others who both played hard on and off the field and were very outspoken. This behavior directly impacted the traditional way of coaching forever — and the way the game has been played since.

A new kind of ball player emerged. Today, the game is more personalized. Athletes even question authority. They want to know *why* a particular exercise or drill has to be carried out and *why* training rules need to be adhered to. Much the same as educators and employers have experienced with students and workers, it has been a time when football coaches had to learn and change to accept the new reality or become ineffective.

Some coaches continue to moan that ball players aren't the same as they used to be. Typical complaints include:

- Players just aren't hungry enough these days.
- Players just aren't as competitive as their fathers used to be.
- Today, if a player finds he's not a star, he just up and quits trying.

It's not so much that the ball players have changed with the times but rather it's the individual coach who may have been unable to keep up. Today, coaches employ a psychology of winning—high energy, be enthusiastic, make it different all the time. Communications is the key. They keep their interaction lively. They keep their players' attention through their competence, confidence and disciplined caring.

SERVICE TO CUSTOMERS: OPHELIMITY THINKING

Ophelimity thinking is customer-centered quality. In football the fan is king (and queen). The team owners are highly sensitive both to fan communication and satisfaction. So are the players.

The TV representatives play their roles exquisitely. The games are presented crisply, colorfully, and accurately—without bias. The announcers, and color men, as often as not, are outstanding ex-players. They point up and convey the intricacies of the game perfectly.

Players spend time signing autographs, appearing on worthwhile projects of service to the community, and often participate in the affairs of their community. Fan approval or disapproval is often the leading cause of turnover, certainly for coaches and occasionally of players.

Players spend time at schools and with the coaches of athletics in schools to recruit fans and create interest in the sport.

Major attempts are made to attract customers and to explain the game so that as many people can understand it and therefore become enthusiastic about it as possible.

All this makes the fundamental definition of quality that is used in virtually every private sector enterprise that is subject to competition: quality is fitness for use as judged by the user—the customer.

CONTINUOUS IMPROVEMENT, BREAKTHROUGH, CONTROL AND A DISCIPLINE OF CARING

Both breakthrough and control are critical to a team's success.

Football illustrates the critical importance of breakthrough and control, separated into squads — *offense* (breakthrough) and *defense* (control). The mindset of the defense is different from the strategy of the offense.

Football is a controlled form of warfare. In football, as in battle, the surest way to success is to outmaneuver the enemy, to penetrate and to secure what has been won. These are the concepts of *breakthrough and control*. The offense is dynamic, decisive movement for penetration — with the intent of scoring. Defense means control.

In warfare the strategy for penetration means seizing the momentum. This is precisely what is used in football.

In contrast, the conceptual approach for defense consists of entrenchment, fortification, and detection. The yard of space which separates the offensive and defensive lines has been described as a "no man's land." It is an apt description; football games are won or lost by control of this narrow slip of land. The battle for it is fought by some of the toughest athletes in the sports world.

Breakthrough and control are part of one continuing cycle of events. The cycle consists of alternating plateaus and gains in performance.

The gains are the result of breakthrough—planned creation of change.
The plateaus are the result of control—preventing change.
This process goes on and on.

Lurking behind this simple truth are some profound differences. First, in terms of leadership and management, control differs remarkably from breakthrough. Successful coaches are fully aware that the attitudes, the organization, and the methodology used to achieve breakthrough differ in essence from those used to achieve control. The differences in fact are so great that the decision of whether, at any one time, to embark on breakthrough, or to continue on control, is of cardinal importance.

Second, continuous improvement links breakthrough and control—small steps open big opportunities. As has been shown in previous chapters, continuous improvement is an American form of what the Japanese culture labels *kaizen*. The concept of American *kaizen* reflects the common law precepts of *Due Care, Due Diligence,* and *Due Regard.* We also see it operate in how coaches, operating through the *playbook* and *pep talks* and *disciplined caring*, essentially follow these steps:

(*1*) They see to it that each player knows what is expected and has an opportunity to influence, but not decide, the results to be achieved.

(*2*) They see to it that assistance is given so that what is expected is most likely to be achieved.

(*3*) They provide feedback so that the player and the team have a clear knowledge of results.

(*4*) They see to it that there is corrective action based on the feedback from the knowledge of results.

(*5*) Through practice, practice, and more practice, they provide many opportunities for success.

Through stories shared in prior chapters, we saw how three elements—continuous improvement, breakthrough, and control—in fact, operate as a *discipline of caring.* Vince Lombardi was baffled by the lackluster performance of his 8th round draft choice and noticed something while reviewing the films from a pre-season exhibition game. Lombardi re-ran the films in slow motion. It soon became evident that Larry Brown was late getting off the ball.

Lombardi had Brown's hearing tested which revealed that his new rookie was deaf in his right ear. Vince Lombardi interceded with then NFL commissioner Pete Rozelle and got permission for a hearing aid to be installed in Brown's helmet.

A coach's ability to spot his player's hearing problem saved the rookie's career. Brown won both the NFL rushing title and was named NFL Player of the Year in 1972.

Expectations, assistance, results, corrective action, and many chances are the "stuff" of *guided learning experience.* They are the fundamental elements of a disciplined form of caring which may require breakthrough, control, and always continuous improvement.

CONTINUOUS USE AND UPGRADING OF TECHNOLOGY

Television gives millions of fans the chance to watch action-packed football and to learn the intricacies of the game. Everywhere one looks, one sees technology in action: Scouting and communication through microphones; filming of the game; even instant replay.

Coaching staffs spend hours every day going over movies of their opponents in action, searching for any flaw in the defense or a telltale giveaway by an offensive player which may tip the defense to a play. Coach Joe Gibbs reminds us: "The biggest learning experience you have is the film. . . . "We're going to take everything we can from the films." From the hours of study come the strategy and tactics of this miniature warfare, and, finally, the staff decisions are translated into checks and circles on a blackboard and enshrined in the playbook, the player's shorthand of football.

Technology—the support elements to American *kaizen*—represents the new "tools of the trade" which has changed the way the game is played. We showed how technology is adapted and upgraded by giving a short history of the evolution of the modern football helmet. The first helmet covered the head with a soft, thin leather that fit snugly and transmitted the shock of a blow almost undiluted. It was once used as a weapon of play until replaced and outlawed by more powerful headgear.

As the game matured and the science of protection progressed with it, the helmets were changed. The leather used was hard leather padded inside. The change helped, but the driving shock of a knee on the side of the helmet, for example, could not be absorbed by such a device. And the Riddell helmet, the prototype of the modern headgear as a plastic shell suspended on webbing, could absorb far more impact. A helmet worn today offers its wearer virtually complete protection from blows to the head.

COACHING AND LEADERSHIP OF SPECIALISTS

Football shows what leaders need to inspire and manage individuals and teams. We have seen how professional football is a game for specialists who must also unite to form a working team. The players can do one thing or a combination of a few things very well. In this array of stars the quarterback must do many things well including lead the offensive team.

From time to time every winning coach wonders "What am I really here for?" Coaches wear lots of hats. The executive role calls for three: leader, manager and administrator. As leader, the coach motivates and supplies the emotional and spiritual essentials of command and inspiration. As administrator, he communicates and enforces the team and league rules and regulations. As manager, he is concerned with the ways his team can achieve breakthrough (offense), control (defense), and continuous improvement (practice, praxis and disciplined caring).

The greatest NFL coaches are teachers. They teach their players how to play the game. They point out to them when things go well. They point out when things did not go so well. Their greatest thrill is to watch the players come together as a team—as a bonding force.

So the coach is really three persons—teacher, father, and friend. Joe Paterno, one of America's best college coaches said it well: "I don't want to pat myself on the back, but I never wanted to be just a football coach. It's important that the faculty understand that I think football has a place in the university, and that the tail's not wagging the dog." *As a teacher*, the coach must take the time and patience to educate these strong and virile young men, not only in the physical skills of the game but also in the mental aspects. As a *father* figure, the coach is the one the player responds to when he fumbles the ball or tosses an intercepted pass. After every play the players look to the coach for feedback—approval and positive body language. Denied this component, the player will soon become confused, disappointed, and unproductive.

Eventually, ball players mature and leave the game. Then, it is especially gratifying when a ball player acknowledges his coach as a *friend* in the bigger game of life. This too is a vital part of the coaching, teaching, and mentoring process.

Sports defines a *professional* leader. It is precisely in answer to this question that the sports metaphor gains much of its power. Each fall millions of Americans spend prime recreation hours (and hours away from work) on hard stadium seats or else glued to television sets and radios, watching or listening to "professional" football. They get a clear demonstration of leadership in action by observing the behavior of owners, coaches and team leaders.

The key to understanding leadership centers on the word professional *as it is used in sports.* Why are the NFL players called professionals? The quick and obvious answer is that they are not amateurs. While true, of course, the term professional in sports means far more than this: it means that they are the best at what they do—*they get results.*

They are *not* called professionals because they complete some prescribed course of instruction. Or graduate from the right college. Or even accumulate a specified number of years of experience. They are *not* professionals because they hold a degree or a certificate or a license to practice. In sports, in stark contrast to leadership in bureaucratic and hierarchical organizations—e.g., government, business and schools—leaders are professionals for one and only one reason. It is their *ability to perform* what is required *to get the intended results.*

Leaders are especially important in dealing with adversity such as with consecutive losing seasons. Good leaders in sports start by dealing directly with and discarding the "old chestnut" encased in institutional memory which says, "This is the way we have always done things around here." Dealing with and breaking old habits calls for a strong leader with vision. Bill Parcells pacing the sidelines or a Joe Torre in the dugout. It requires attention to the playbook to lay out the alternative actions that point to basic improvements.

COOPETITION: SIMULTANEOUS COLLABORATION AND COMPETITION

Collaboration or competition, the standard dichotomy, the prevailing either-or, is exposed in professional football as a false dichotomy, one no longer suited for a changing world economy. In sports, as in a global economy, it is not either/or but both.

We have shown the reasons for both collaboration and competition in previous chapters—particularly by showing how the introduction of the *free agent* has served to keep the football teams balanced and exciting for fans by not allowing any one time to be forever dominant.

Does coopetition work? Sometimes yes, sometimes no. Coopetition is a mindset driven by the overriding objective that *mutual success* is the superior and most desirable result.

The NFL model is an excellent example. Each week the teams battle it out (compete) on the playing field trying to reach that championship season. The owners recognize the intrinsic value of their franchise—

which only is as good as its support from the fans. It is the fan—the customer—who is king. The owners have crafted a system (cooperation) of teams, conferences, playoffs, player drafts, and free agents to level the competition. The sport provides a simulation of life and death warfare (competition). Each performance is seen by thousands of fans in a multi-million dollar stadium as well as seen by millions each week on TV as games rotate on the sports networks (cooperation). It is all top draw entertainment. At its foundation is a big sports entertainment business—which has evolved through mutual need and trust as a model of *coopetition*.

Once hard and fast distinctions between competitors, customers, and suppliers have now given way to new circumstances and situations. The spawning of *coopetition* is part cooperator/collaborator and part competitor. With unprecedented economic shift competitive boundaries are continuously moving and converging. Successfully running new play patterns through this emerging chaos requires enterprise to continually reevaluate where and what type of "focused competencies" it needs to be competitive. Vexing questions are raised.

Coopetition then surfaces as the only reasonable approach to holding your own in the new and brutally competitive, yet necessarily collaborative, global economy. *Coopetition* requires loyalty among competitors—trust, craftsmanship and cooperation, as well as power sharing among employees.

Teamwork is a feature of human capital development. The constant winners in football display a near perfect combination of speed, power, and versatility that comes from the bonds formed among the players forged through teamwork. Years of working together and facing the climate pressure that is the life of every player, have made the regulars almost intuitive in their knowledge of each other's reactions. They both compete and collaborate with one another (the hallmark of coopetition)—the competition is to be better, the collaboration exists when the team is at Game Time.

PRAXIS MAKES PERFECT

We introduced 33 examples of good practice in education to show that there are "plays" in that arena that, by analogy, are like the ones in sports. Praxis is the word that means the know-how, the "what works" in a given profession or occupation. When we say that the physician has a medical practice, we don't mean that he or she is learning how to be a physician. We do mean that he or she is competent, i.e., knows how to treat patients and is actually doing his or her work as a physician. The playbook contains the praxis of football, the "what works" that is so crucial to winning and playing the game well.

Football has a large assortment of coaches — line and backfield coaches to name but two. They constantly revisit the fundamentals to assure team balance. They look for breakthroughs, control and continuous improvement. Development coaches are specialists. They teach the art of finding breakthrough ideas. They also target control. In this coaching scenario practical *development* and *achievement* are *seamless*.

If players are concerned about their assignments they'll have a tendency to hold back. They need to be so familiar with the playbook and their assignments that when the game starts, they're running on auto-pilot — such as each of us experiences when we drive a car. When players are not distracted they can let go and do what the job calls for.

Don Shula puts it this way: ". . . This is why the playbook everybody gets at training camp is so important," he said. "Everything they need to know about their position is in there."

Instruction, as coaches actually perform the role, is an orderly and systematic one. Its most important feature is that it must lead to *demonstrated* learning. To the coach, instruction has a central purpose: improving learning — learning focused on specific results. The playbook is a valuable instrument for achieving what is desired. From the sports perspective, then, instruction is a special kind of teaching. It may be possible to say that teaching may be what teachers do; coaching is what the learner does.

In sports, there's a big difference among the administrative and content decisions a coach makes and the decisions he makes that deal with instruction. Administrative and content decisions are large, they emphasize *what* to do. The instructional decisions are narrower, they deal with *how* to implement the other decisions.

For instruction, the coach asks himself and others "How best can we assure learning?" *How* decisions cause a careful search of the available praxis — the storehouse of good practice for results. *How* decisions summon experimentation and try-out to see if they actually work. Experimentation, feedback and empirical evidence are the essence of good coaching in the improvement of individual player and team performance. They are also the heart of instruction.

PRACTICE MAKES PERFECT

Training in football is never-ending both before, during, and after the season. The difference between victory and defeat, barring the flukes of chance, will depend on what first takes place on a simple patch of grass, sometimes adjacent to the stadium, surrounded by a functional looking chain link fence shrouded with black tarpaulin for security and a few bleachers. It is there, away from the stadium glitter and lights, that the success of your team will, in large part, be first determined.

On that patch of grass there will be sweat, hits, and endless repetition. Success starts gradually. The backbone of the winning team is forged in the seemingly endless hours of practice, practice, and still more practice, together with careful evening study of the playbook.

For the rookie who makes the team, a new trial begins. Mistakes which were condoned in practice or in exhibition games draw quick and bitter censure now from teammates and from coaches. The arsenal of plays which arms a pro team on offense or defense is staggering. It takes long hours of study for the rookie to master assignments which have become second nature to the old pros on the team.

Then there are the technical subtleties of football – the techniques of blocking and tackling and running which college coaches lacked the time or the knowledge to explain. There is a never-ending study of the players on the other teams. The rookie becomes a member of a team within a team. For a while, he'll probably play on the "suicide squad" – the special team which kicks off or receives the kickoff. As time and injuries wear away the starting offensive and defensive platoons, he'll earn a place on one of them. A pro team is two teams, separate and distinct, with different coaches, different skills, different things to learn.

As the year winds down into December, he'll find he's no longer a rookie, except in name. His education as a pro is still far from complete; it will never be complete. In the season five or more years away when he finally leaves the sport, he will probably feel, as many old pros feel, that he is quitting just as he is truly learning how to play football.

What happens for championship games shows the importance of continuous learning and the need for constant practice. On the same field where a particular game time will take place, players meticulously prepare for the game. The players clad in sweat suits, begin the precise choreography of football, tracing plays over and over again. The field is a rehearsal area with the coaches translating their scouting into an attack plan, then drilling the troops in plan execution.

Consider the following elements of the sport. Grind it out, yard by yard. Control and start again. Memorize your playbook. The basic strategy for winning – wear down your opponent. Do more things right and force the other guys to make more mistakes.

Through careful study of learning by scholars, we know a great deal about how people learn effectively. Coaches put this knowledge into action both personally and through the playbook. We also know the best conditions under which people can apply their knowledge to new situations and it challenges what still goes on today in many schools and colleges. Coaches know that effective learning experience needs to: (1) Be organized to deliver learning efficiently; (2) Reflect knowledge and experience-based demands and game time contexts in which knowledge and skills have to be used; (3) Develop knowledge and skills that are both broadly and specifically applicable; and therefore (4) Blur the division between what educators might call academic and vocational learning.

Training in sports builds upon: (1) what people need to know and the know how to do it, and (2) how people learn most naturally and effectively.

SCHOOL IMPROVEMENT RECOMMENDATIONS FROM SOME OF AMERICA'S MOST KNOWLEDGEABLE STAKEHOLDERS AND PRACTITIONERS

Following are powerful ideas for inclusion in your playbook. Dr. John Murphy, then Superintendent of Schools of Charlotte, North Carolina, and today home of the Carolina Panthers, the most successful new franchise in NFL history, is one of America's truly outstanding education practitioners. In the early 1990's, Dr. Murphy assembled a panel of some of America's most outstanding educational stakeholders and leaders to get their recommendations for producing a world-class school system. The names and a brief description of each of the panel members follows.

(*1*) **William Bennett,** former national "drug czar" and U.S. Secretary of Education, currently a John M. Olin senior fellow at the Hudson Institute

(*2*) **Ernest Boyer,** president of the Carnegie Foundation for the Advancement of Teaching

(*3*) **James Comer,** education writer and senior fellow at the Hudson Institute

(*4*) **Chester Finn, Jr.,** professor of education and public policy at Vanderbilt University and director of the Education Excellence Network

(*5*) **Patricia Graham,** president of the Spencer Foundation and professor of History of American Education at Harvard University

(*6*) **Matina Horner,** former president of Radcliffe College and currently executive vice president of Teachers Insurance and Annuity Association – College Retirement Equities Fund

(*7*) **James Kelly,** president and chief executive officer of the National Board of Professional Teaching Standards

(*8*) **John Slaughter,** president of Occidental College

(*9*) **Donald Stewart,** president of the College Board

Leon Lessinger, a long-time friend and colleague of Dr. Murphy, was invited to listen in on the panel's discussion. Lessinger has long written about, spoken about and advocated similar recommendations. He had the benefit of hearing what the panel concluded as well as receiving an advanced draft of their written recommendations.

Major aspects of the panel's findings, which follow, illustrate some of the best thinking currently available from some of the best minds in education for sparking productive discussions for improving education. We have discovered that one powerful way to prepare for developing your playbook is by working with stakeholders and having them address the recommendations using the following six "thinking prompts":

(*1*) What's good or bad or just plain interesting about each of the recommendations?

(*2*) Has the panel considered all the important factors?

(*3*) What alternatives, possibilities and choices are there?

(*4*) How would the different constituents of the schools view the recommendations?

(*5*) What is the first priority . . . the second, and so forth?

(*6*) What consequences might there be because of the adoption of a particular recommendation in the short term and in the longer term?

INSIGHTS FROM THE PANEL: THEIR ORGANIZING PRINCIPLES

To create a "world-class" organization—one which is client-centered with a *passion for results*—there are 10 organizing principles. Together, they erect a sturdy framework for change.

- First. Set high standards of intellectual attainment which we require all schools to produce and all young people to reach. For too long, too little has been expected of both.
- Second. Organize the system around those cognitive outcomes. It's time to reorient schools so they focus on results, not on rules and procedures.
- Third. The school system must respond to differences in children and their social, cultural and economic realities in ways that enable all students to learn the identified core of knowledge.
- Fourth. Certain consequences—pleasant or not—must follow success or failure to meet the stated outcomes. Schooling is an enterprise that treats all its staff exactly alike, no matter how they perform.
- Fifth. While goals should be set centrally, the means to reach them must be the domain of professionals at the building level. Edicts from on high must stop.
- Sixth. Effective, prompt and accurate ways to measure progress toward meeting the stated goals must be developed at the district level.
- Seventh. The inclination to protect the status quo must give way to a spirit of innovation and experimentation—and it is those qualities—not politics which must govern professional advancements within the system.
- Eighth. We must put our money where our mouths are and

bring spending in line with the new priorities. That means shifting resources that currently support administrative functions to the front lines to bolster the education of children.

- Ninth. There are no shortcuts. To do more and do better, students, staff and parents will have to invest more time and energy to education.
- Tenth. Schools cannot do the job alone. As panelist Ernest Boyer stated "You cannot build an island of excellence in a sea of indifference."

PANEL RECOMMENDATIONS

There are three things to decide about each proposed strategy. One, is it worth implementing? Two, if so, when? And three, is it an idea that should be imposed universally or piloted first?

- (1) **Standards and Expectations:** "The panel recommends the adoption of high, rigorous and measurable standards for academic performance which reflect global demands and require all students to meet them. We live in a world of determined, well-educated competitors. Our students must match the competition which resides in Bonn, Stockholm, Paris, Seoul and Osaka or our destiny is no longer assured."

- (2) **The Diploma:** "The panel recommends making the diploma meaningful. Currently, most high school diplomas mean only that a student has accumulated seat time in an approved locations—more a clue to patience than evidence of authentic academic achievement. Employers don't trust it and students know it has little bearing on their future plans."

- (3) **Curriculum:** "The panel recommends the overhaul of curriculum to provide a nourishing menu of courses consistent with the new standards. The proliferation of options means a graduate can escape the system having digested a handful of diluted courses in math, the sciences, history and the languages. Only about 30 percent of the students take algebra, and only 38 percent complete a foreign language. Our students aren't learning things today because they are not studying them."

- (4) **Curricular Tracking:** "The panel recommends eliminating the current curricular tracking system which gives the 'good' students one curriculum and the 'poor' students a watered-down version. Those unfortunate enough to be dumped into the general or vocational tracks – systems characterized by unchallenging courses and the accumulation of low-level skills – find themselves unprepared for either post-secondary education or meaningful work. It perpetuates a cruel hoax on students."

(5) **Values, Work and Citizenship:** "The panel recommends that schools get back to teaching democratic values, work and citizenship competencies. Values tell us what is important and unimportant; the difference between right and wrong. Devotion to the virtues of liberty, equality, justice, compassion, charity and duty are integral to our concept of citizenship just as punctuality, honesty, trustworthiness and civility are to the values of the workplace. A diverse, pluralistic nation needs a population grounded in a solid core of knowledge and skills. It also needs a people united by a shared set of ethical and democratic values."

(6) **Time:** "The panel recommends letting students proceed at their own pace, giving them as much or as little time as they need to acquire the required skills and knowledge – understanding that everyone will be held to the same high standard in order to graduate. It is time to erase the unrealistic, misguided assumption that all youngsters can learn the same amount during a six-hour, 180-day school year. Keep in mind that as long as young people in other nations commit a far greater share of their lives to schooling, it is doubtful our students' academic accomplishments will equal theirs."

(7) **Testing:** "The panel recommends teaching to the tests – to new performance type assessment measures – that assess curricula in rich form and pose serious intellectual challenges for students. So long as we look to test results for student learning, tests should be worth teaching to."

(8) **Technology:** "The panel recommends that the school system take full advantage of technology's potential. Technology revolutionizes schooling because it makes learning portable. It means that learning and all things connected to schooling need not occur in a classroom, six feet from the teacher's desk."

(9) **Ready to Learn:** "The panel recommends getting to children early – at birth – to help prepare them for the future. To improve

schools, a solid foundation must be laid. If children do not have a good beginning, it is difficult to compensate fully for society's failure later on in their lives. Recent estimates are that nearly 35 percent of the nation's children come to school not fully ready to participate successfully in kindergarten."

(*10*) **At-Risk Students:** "The panel recommends that specific strategies be implemented to target young people whose life circumstances put them at risk of letting go or losing out. Although some may be able to escape on their own, a larger percentage will need special attention if they are to have a decent chance at joining the mainstream. These young people are in danger of a lot more than failing at school. With their very lives at stake theirs is not a condition that schools alone can solve."

(*11*) **Teaching:** "The panel recommends a series of strategies to make teaching a more rewarding and respected profession, to improve the preparation and performance of teachers and to secure expert personnel for the schools. Today not enough academically able students are being attracted to teaching; "good" teachers and "not so good" teachers are treated exactly alike. The professional working lives of teachers can be best characterized as 'blue-collar,' and in-service programs are one big yawn."

(*12*) **Reapportioning Power:** "The panel recommends a radical shift in power to the front lines of education. School-house professionals should be free to organize themselves subject only to a simple market test of student success as defined by the system. Once academic standards are clearly identified, schools need to be cut loose to decide how best to get the job done for their students. Borrowing from businesses which have catapulted to the top of their trades, the principles of autonomy, flexibility, competition, and accountability must reign supreme."

(*13*) **Parents:** "The panel recommends paying as much attention to improving parenting and parental relations as reforming schools. Parents make a huge difference in how much and how well their children learn and are the majority shareholder of the time children spend out of school. Parents are, therefore, schools' most important partners in facilitating and reinforcing students' "jobs" to work hard to learn challenging subject matter. It's time to invest properly in the relationship and stop trying to do it on the cheap."

(*14*) **Community Support:** "The panel recommends that the community pitch in. Estimates are that 91 percent of youngsters' lives are spent outside of school. Parents, churches, social welfare organizations, employers, and a variety of other institutions are the custodians of that time. That means responsibility for educating children does not—cannot—belong to teachers and schools alone."

IMPLEMENTING STRATEGIES

It's time to get serious about a winning performance. Ask local employers and colleges to hold students accountable by creating real consequences for doing well in school and real consequences for doing poorly. If there are no real-life consequences to not performing well, students are not likely to put forth the effort. For instance, how about reducing tuition for good students or paying them an extra dollar an hour? At the least, we should set high, rigorous and specific standards for employment or college entrance, and stick to them. If there are no real life consequences to not performing well, students won't put forth the effort. Would you?

Enlist the help of the press. Ask the newspaper and television station to dedicate a daily section to education just as they do to sports. Unless the community unites to elevate the status of schooling, there is little chance for widespread improvement.

It takes a community effort. . . . Mobilize the community to provide early childhood services, whether they be in the form of programs at libraries, museums, zoos and shopping malls or affordable day care.

Involve those who can really benefit from better schools. Ask businesses to open their doors to students for vocational training and community service opportunities and to teachers for staff development.

If you *really* want parent support in the schools make it easy for parents to get involved. Urge employers to grant parents leave time to volunteer in schools, attend parent conferences, and regularly communicate with their children's schools.

Don't be shy. Draw upon your community's human assets. Sign up volunteer mentors to fulfill the pledge to give every energetic and deserving child that critical extra boost needed for success.

Take the lead. Ask the community how it can create neighborhoods for learning. Schools would guide, not provide these services.

Apply the same principles to yourself and your community as you would to students. Produce an annual report card on how well the community is doing.

MEASURES OF SUCCESS

Your education scoreboard is now ready to measure your teams' results and the effectiveness of your playbook. The following academic achievement outcomes, student participation rates and customer satisfaction ratings will serve as your benchmarks of success.

Students demonstrate competency over challenging subject matter in the five core areas of math, English, science, history and geography as measured by the new criterion-referenced tests and a host of authentic assessments.

The percentage of students who score in the top quartiles of national assessments in science, history and geography increases significantly, and the distribution of minority students more closely reflects the student population as a whole.

On national assessments in which the students can participate, students *lead the nation* in reading and computational skills by the turn of the century.

On international comparisons in which the students can participate on other measures of rigor such as SAT and ACT, students *score well above the national average*.

The number of students who are competent in a second language *increases substantially*.

The number of students meeting International Baccalaureate and/or Advanced Placement standards *doubles in three years*.

The percentage of preschoolers coming to school ready to learn *rises significantly each year*.

Students take a rigorous college preparatory course of study, including algebra and geometry. Students who enter the apprenticeship or the "Two-plus-two" program are *successful in securing high-skill jobs* upon graduation.

College *acceptance rates* of poor and minority children, *skyrocket*.

The *dropout rate drops* dramatically over time. The *gap* in high school graduation rates between black and white students is *eliminated*.

Suspension and exclusion rates drop significantly at every level of schooling and the gap between black and white suspensions is eliminated.

ON THE SCALE OF SATISFACTION

The goal is:

- To score parent satisfaction with schools high.
- To score employer satisfaction with students high.
- To score student performance in the first year of college above average.

IN CONCLUSION

We hope our readers now see in the world of sports a potential winning perspective that can be added to every educator's mindset. We chose the title of our book to be *Game Time: The Educator's Playbook for the New Global Economy* because we wanted to show how a discussion of American professional sports—particularly NFL football—lights up the dark corners of obstacles to becoming successful in today's changing global economy.

It should be clear by now that the authors really are *optimists-by-design*—pragmatists who seek answers, not excuses, to problems. That is the reason we think of the interaction with a playbook as solution talk. We know that in professional sports, every season is a new season, with new opportunities for winning. In every season, there are additions, modifications, and deletions to last year's playbook; constant revision takes advantage of what has been learned and what may have changed.

To repeat many of the most successful coaches in football, there is no single magic playbook. If there was, everyone would run the same plays all of the time. There is no magic way to do things. There are many different ways to do things. Your playbook will capture your knowledge, your experience, and your creativity.

Our book was intended as a thoughtful guide to praxis, to "what works" to meet the changing and increasingly tough situations brought on by a fiercely competitive global economy. Now, that condition has become both an "enemy" and a source of opportunity.

SCANS Report Summary

IN 1989, THE Secretary of Labor and members of what was called the *Secretary's Commission on Achieving Necessary Skills* (SCANS), published a set of world-class work force standards as concerned representatives of the nation's schools, businesses, unions, and government. The standards reflected their examination of the major changes in the world of work and the implications of those changes for learning.

They clearly understood that schools do more than simply prepare people to make a living. Thus their report concerns only one part of that education, the part that involves how schools prepare young people for work. It does not deal with other, equally important, concerns that are also the proper responsibility of our educators.

The report points out that for most of this century, as this nation took its goods and know-how to the world, America did not have to worry about competition from abroad. At home, the technology of mass production emphasized discipline to the assembly line. Today, the report argues, the demands on business and workers are different. Firms must meet world-class standards and so must workers. Employers seek adaptability and the ability to learn and work in teams.

This change has many implications. The focus is on the more than half of our young people who leave school without the knowledge or foundation required to find and hold a good job. The report warns that unless all work to turn this situation around, these young people, and those who employ them, will pay a very high price. Low skills lead to low wages and low profits. Many of these youth will never be able to earn a decent living. And, in the long run, this will damage severely the quality of life everyone hopes to enjoy.

The Commission spent 12 months talking to business owners, to public employers, to the people who manage employees daily, to union officials, and to workers on the line and at their desks. They talked to them in their stores, shops, government offices, and manufacturing facilities. Their message was the same across the country and in every kind of job. good jobs depend on people who can put knowledge to work. New workers must be creative and responsible problem solvers and have the skills and attitudes on which employers can build. Traditional jobs are changing and new jobs are created everyday. High paying but unskilled jobs are disappearing. Employers and employees share the belief that all workplaces must "work smarter."

From these conversations, they drew three major conclusions.

All American high school students must develop a new set of competencies and foundation skills if they are to enjoy a productive, full, and satisfying life. Whether they go next to work, apprenticeship, the armed services, or college, all young Americans should leave high school with the know-how they need to make their way in the world. In the SCANS report, know-how has two parts: competence and a foundation of skills and personal qualities. Less than one-half of our young people possess it. They predicted that this know-how will be important to those who will be developing the World-Class Standards for educational performance.

The report emphasizes that the qualities of high performance that today characterize our most competitive companies must become the standard for the vast majority of our companies, large and small, local and global. By "high performance" they mean work settings relentlessly committed to excellence, product quality, and customer satisfaction.

They declare that these goals are pursued by combining technology and people in new ways. Decisions must be made closer to the frontline and draw upon the abilities of workers to think creatively and solve problems. Above all, these goals depend on people—on managers committed to high performance and to the competence of their work force and on responsible employees comfortable with technology and complex systems, skilled as members of teams, and with a passion for continuous learning.

The nation's schools must be transformed into high-performance organizations in their own right. Despite a decade of reform efforts, the findings of the report demonstrate little improvement in student achievement.

The report says, "We are failing to develop the full academic abilities of most students and utterly failing the majority of poor, disadvantaged, and minority youngsters. By transforming the nation's schools into high-performance organizations, we mean schools relentlessly committed to producing skilled graduates as the norm, not the exception."

The report identifies five competencies, which, in conjunction with a three-part foundation of skills and personal qualities, lie at the heart of job performance today. These eight areas represent essential preparation *for all students*, both those going directly to work and those planning further education. All eight must be an integral part of every young person's school life.

Seldom does one of these eight components stand alone in job performance.

They are highly integrated, and most tasks require workers to draw on several of them.

The report has a serious message for employers as well as educators. Employers must orient their business practices to hiring and developing this know-how in employees. If they do not develop a world-class work force, the report argues, "your business inevitably will be at risk."

Here is what they suggest employers can do. "First, reorganize your workplace into the high-performance environment of the future. Nine out of ten employers are operating on yesterday's workplace assumption. Do not be one of them. Second, invest in your employees so that they can obtain the skills needed to succeed in this new environment. Third, tell educators clearly what you need and work with them to accomplish it. You know that students have to believe that you care about what they learn. Employers who value performance in high school when they make their hiring decisions provide students with the right signal: learning and earning are related activities."

Educators have to instill in students the perspective on results that the SCANS skills demand. If they do not, they will be failing their students and the community as they try to adjust to the next century. "You, more than anyone," the report says, "are responsible for helping our children develop the skills they need."

Here is how they argue educators can help. "First, tell your students what the standards are—what is expected of them. Second, give them the benefit of a fair and firm assessment of where they stand and what they need to do. If they pass from grade to grade and receive diplomas without mastering these skills, they cannot make their way in the world of work. Third, inject the competencies and the foundation we have defined into every nook and cranny of the school curriculum. Your most gifted students need this know-how, and so do those experiencing the greatest difficulties in the classroom. We are convinced that if students are taught the know-how in the context of relevant problems, you will find them more attentive, more interested—indeed, more teachable—because they will find the coursework challenging and relevant."

Generalized Universal Model of American Kaizen *for Use in Developing Human Capital in Homes, Schools, and Workplaces on a Continuous Basis*

AMERICAN *KAIZEN* IS a process for developing and enriching human capital through guided learning experience in the context of proactivity and skilled caring. The universal process applying due care, due diligence, and due regard is as follows:

Step 1: Share Expectations
Communicate what each person is expected to know and be able to do to be successful.

Step 2: Listen Carefully to Concerns about Expectations
Let the person comment on each expectation, and, if feasible, adjust the expectation to fit a concern.

Step 3: Use What Works as Assistance
Provide assistance in meeting each expectation by using good practice – (tested knowledge and technology) what works – as the basis of your assistance.

Step 4: Let People Know Results
Provide timely feedback through agreed upon assessment methods to show him or her how well or how poorly the expectations are being met.

Step 5: Plan Again for Success, Not Failure
For each poorly met expectation, develop a joint plan for corrective action.

Step 6: Assist the Person to Successfully Meet the New Plan
Repeat Steps 1–4, if necessary, while he or she enacts the corrective action plan.

Step 7:   Be Patient and Let Him or Her Try Again
Give him or her many chances to succeed. Repeat the entire process if necessary. Experience has demonstrated that most people succeed in meeting the expectations processed through American *kaizen*. Not all are successful; far fewer will fail.

This sequence of steps that are the major factors in the American *kaizen* guided learning experience process fit all situations where mastery of skill and knowledge is involved. They are truly universals on how to care in a skilled way for students, followers, constituents, clients, and customers.

Guided Learning Principles

SCHOOLS THAT ARE WINNERS

- Make students and parents part of a school choice process.
- Give teachers wide latitude to create, change, excel; reward performance.
- Use smaller school sizes; acquire surplus space suitable for additional school usage.
- Assign a personal mentor to each student; a 500 to 1 student counseling system is obsolete.
- Nurture parent participation; the school requires their involvement. Both are essential.
- Stop everything for a parent conference, making it easy for the parents to get involved.
- Center on depth in teaching since basics and critical thinking are prerequisites.
- Reassign costs to more line workers to achieve lower student/teacher ratios.
- Put money where the need is: on the line with more teachers.

Just as business moves to the horizontal organization to get closer to its customer, the same holds true for schools, and collaboration between education and jobs is essential.

ACTIONS LINKING SCHOOLS AND ENTERPRISE

- Build community-wide apprenticeship programs for noncollege-bound youths based on the economic characteristics of your local economy. Search out those alternatives that help build local and regional economic strength.

- Have enterprise assist schools in determining the stress areas in math, science, reading, as well as attitude and behavior. A job at McDonald's or Burger King, Federal Express or UPS now requires a combination of people skills and high-tech comfort for ordering and cash collection.
- Think globally, act locally. All school output must eventually meet the challenge of global competition. Think neighborhood by neighborhood, school by school.
- Search out and develop the many excellent examples of cutting-edge teaching and learning methods already in use that can be replicated throughout the system. This issue is too important to rely on the heroics of an isolated teacher, principal, or school.
- Get enterprise working with the schools. Send grades to internship firms as well as home. Give students incentives to excel and perform.
- Rethink early student tracking. For too long now these have been used more for teaching convenience than student benefit. Open up creativity; learning will blossom.

BENCHMARKS FOR ENTERPRISE

- Seek out and adopt updated standards for self-improvement.
- Develop a work force team effort. We're all in the global economic game together.
- Grant power to the employee to stop the line if it isn't right for the customer.
- Encourage employee ideas and employee ownership in implementing those ideas.
- Commit your company to be a learning company.
- Provide continuous training and education during each employee's entire career.
- Show initiative by involving customers in your product or service strategies.
- Team with competitors to identify and solve larger problems.

The learning commonwealth is an environment where people, policies, strategies, and actions are in a constant state of renewal. It creates a community of shared interests, shared capital (both intellectual and monetary), and shared risks.

Aguayo, Rafael. 1990. *Dr. Deming: The American Who Taught the Japanese About Quality.* New York: Simon & Schuster.

Albrecht, Karl. 1992. *The Only Thing That Matters: Bring the Power of the Customer into the Center of Your Business.* New York: Harper Business.

Allen, George. 1990. *Strategies for Winning.* New York, NY: McGraw-Hill.

American Association of School Administrators. 1992. *Creating Quality Schools.* Arlington, VA: AASA.

American Association of School Administrators. 1991. *An Introduction to Total Quality for Schools: A Collection of Articles on the Concepts of Total Quality Management and W. Edwards Deming.* Arlington, VA: AASA.

American Demographics. The Free Agent. 1993 October; Internet research.

Bandura, A. 1986. From thought to action: Mechanisms of personal agency. *New Zealand Journal of Psychology.* 15, 1–17.

Bandura, A. 1986. *Social Foundations of Thought and Action: A Social-Cognitive Theory.* Englewood Cliffs, NJ: Prentice-Hall.

Bates, Richard. 1981. "Management and the Culture of the School." In *Management of Resources in Schools: Study Guide I,* edited by Richard Bates and Course Team. Geelong, Australia: Deakin University.

Berryman, Sue E. and Bailey, Thomas R. 1992. *The Double Helix of Education and the Economy.* New York: The Institute of Education and the Economy, Teachers College, Columbia University.

Bogan, C. E. and English, M. J. 1994. *Benchmarking for Best Practices: Winning through Innovative Adaptation.* New York, NY: McGraw-Hill, Inc.

Bryce, J. and Polick, B. 1985. *Power Basics of Football.* Englewood Cliffs, NJ: Prentice-Hall.

Cairnes, H. 1949. "The Student Objectives," *Lancet* ii, 665.

Commission on the Skills of the American Workplace. 1989. *America's Choice: High Wages or Low Skills!* National Center for Education and the Economy.

Covey, Stephen R. 1991. *Principle-Centered Leadership.* New York: Summit Books.

Crawford, Richard. 1991. *In the Era of Human Capital.* New York: Harper Collins.

Davidow, William H. and Bro Uttal. 1989. *Total Customer Service: The Ultimate Weapon.* New York: Harper & Row.

Davis, S. and Botkin, J. 1994. *The Monster Under the Bed.* New York, NY: Touchstone Books.

Deal, Terrence E. and Kennedy, Allen A. 1982. *Corporate Cultures: The Rite and Rituals of Corporate Life.* Reading, MA: Addison-Wesley Publishing Company.

Deming, W. Edwards. 1992. *Quality, Productivity, and Competitive Position.* Handbook for Seminar. Atlanta, Georgia: September 1–4, 1992.

Drake, Telbert L. and Roe, William H. 1986. *The Principalship,* 3rd Edition. New York: McMillan Publishing Company.

Drucker, Peter. 1971. *Men, Ideas & Politics.* New York: Harper & Row.

Drucker, P. F. 1973. *Management.* New York, NY: Harper & Row.

Drucker, Peter. 1993. *Post-Capitalist Society.* New York: Harper Business.

Forrester, Jay W. 1975. *Collected Papers of Jay W. Forrester.* Cambridge, MA, Wright-Allen Press, Inc.

Franklin, B. 1964. *The Autobiography of Benjamin Franklin* (Annotated). New Haven, CT: Yale University Press.

Gardner, H. 1985. *The Mind's New Science.* New York: Basic Books.

Gates, B. 1995. *The Road Ahead.* New York, NY: Penguin Books.

Halberstam, David. 1993. *The Fifties.* New York: Villard Books.

Hession, J. and Lynch, K. 1994. *War Stories from the Field,* San Francisco, CA: Foghorn Press.

Herrigel, E. 1953. *Zen in the Art of Archery.* New York, NY: Pantheon Books.

Howard, P. K. 1994. *The Death of Common Sense.* New York, NY: Random Press.

Jenkins, Sally. 1991. "Racket Science," *Sports Illustrated,* Time Inc. April 29, p. 72.

Juran, J. M. 1974. "Basic Concepts," *Quality Control Handbook,* Third Edition. New York: McGraw-Hill.

Lessinger, Leon. 1971. *Every Kid a Winner.* New York: Simon & Schuster.

Lessinger, Leon. April 1980. "The Exercise of Due Care in Education: Towards Standards of Professional Practice." *Educational Technology,* pp. 15–19.

Lessinger, Leon. 1993–94. "Attracting Customers to Public Schools." *National Forum of Teacher Education Journal,* V. 3, No. 1.

Lessinger, Leon. April 1994. "Towards a National Educational Extension Service," *International Journal of Educational Reform,* V. 3, No. 2.

Master Plan for Florida Post-secondary Education for the 21st century (September 22, 1993). *Challenges, Realities, Strategies.* Post-secondary Planning Commission.

McCullough, David. 1992. *Truman.* New York: Simon & Schuster.

Meyerhoff, Milton. 1971. *On Caring.* New York: Harper & Row.

Nuwer, H. 1988. *Strategies of the Great Coaches.* New York, NY: Franklin Watts.

Parcells, B. 1996. Finding a Way to Win. *U.S. Air Magazine,* February.

Peabody, W. 1927. "The Care of the Patient." *JAMA,* pp. 877–882.

Peters, T. J. and Waterman, R. H., Jr. 1982. *In Search of Excellence.* New York: Harper & Row.

Powell, Colin M. with Persico, Joseph E. 1995. *An American Journey.* New York: Random House.

Riley, P. 1993. *The Winner Within.* New York, NY: G. P. Putnam's Sons.

The Secretary's Commission on Achieving Necessary Skills, *What Work Requires of Schools: A SCANS Report for America 2000* (June, 1991). U.S. Department of Labor.

Schoor, G. 1987. *100 Years of Notre Dame Football.* William Morrow and Company, Inc.

Senge, P. 1990. *The Fifth Discipline.* New York, NY: Doubleday.

Shaskin, Marshall & Kiser, Kenneth J. 1993. *Putting Total Quality Management to Work.* San Francisco: Berrett-Koehler.

Shula, D. and Blanchard, K. 1995. *Everyone's a Coach.* New York, NY: Harper Business.

Spencer, Herbert. 1873. *Education: Intellectual, Moral & Physical.* New York: D. Appleton & Co.

Stein, H. 1996. Good Times, Bad Vibes. *The Wall Street Journal.* March 14.

Taylor, Frederick W. 1967. *The Principles of Scientific Management.* New York: The Norton Library (originally published in 1911).

Thurow, L. 1992. *Head to Head.* New York, NY: William Morrow and Company.

Thurow, L. 1996. *The Future of Capitalism.* New York: William Morrow and Company.

Waitley, D. 1995. *Empires of the Mind.* New York, NY: William Morrow and Company.

Waterman, R. H. Jr. 1990. *Adhocracy.* New York, NY: WW Norton and Company.

Leon M. Lessinger

Leon M. Lessinger, Ed.D., Eminent Scholar of Education Policy and Economic Development, University of North Florida, is a Senior Fellow of the Florida Institute of Education, former Chair, Board of Governors, Florida Educational Research & Development Program. He received his B.S. in Mechanical Engineering from North Carolina State, B.A. in Psychology, and M.Ed. and Ed.D. in Educational Psychology/Administration from UCLA. He holds an Honorary Doctorate in Science from La Verne College, California. Dr. Lessinger was chosen by Vice President Hubert Humphrey to launch the National Teachers Corps, served as President of the Aerospace Education Foundation, and Associate Commissioner for Elementary and Secondary Education in the U.S. Office of Education. Formerly Dean of the College of Education, University of South Carolina, Clinical Professor of Medicine at UCLA, and Superintendent of three California school districts, he has published widely and is a California licensed psychologist.

Allen E. Salowe

Allen E. Salowe, AICP, is a Consultant/Educator and Senior Fellow of the Florida Institute of Education (State University System) at the University of North Florida and Senior Fellow of the Florida Center for Electronic Communication at Florida Atlantic University. He received his B.A. in Economics from the University of Miami and his M.B.A. in Management from Nova University. He served as President of the Plainfield (NJ) School Board, managed university-based urban policy studies, and is Adjunct Professor of Graduate Studies at Webster University. He was formerly senior operations executive for ITT Consumer Services Group; Sr. VP Planning for ITT Community Development Corporation; Group Planning Director, Champion International; and cofounder of VTI, a computer animation firm. He presently serves as Economist and Financial Adviser to Florida special taxing districts. Mr. Salowe is a member of the American Institute of Certified Planners.